MW00745079

PEACE *with the*

RESTLESS

ME

PEACE

with the
RESTLESS ME

Janice W. Hearn

WORD BOOKS, Publisher
Waco, Texas

TO

NEAL
who cared enough to stay with me
when "for better or worse" meant worse

STEVE, DIANE AND SHARON
who are teaching me how to mother

LOU AND COKE
who made the introductions and held my hand
until the relationship with Christ was secure

In Appreciation

I AM DEEPLY grateful for the persons God has placed along my pathway. Those who have touched my life with the tender loving care of Christ have participated in the making of this book. They've helped to change my life story through a multitude of precious gifts—a gentle word spoken, an arm about my shoulder, a casserole, a bouquet of flowers. Fellow writers at Mount Hermon Christian Writers Conference and those in my Penwomen's group have urged me on. Others have ministered to me through sermons and books which gave new insights.

Some have helped in very specific ways. My friend Christy Zatkin has shared the hope and the apprehensions from the first day I dared to speak of my dream. Ralph Osborne gave me the certainty of knowing writing is a gift of the Spirit. Keith Miller's willingness to answer a letter from an unknown fan gave me courage to begin, and direction in the form of a writing course at the University of

Oklahoma. Gretchen Janssen encouraged me when I believed myself too ordinary to say anything important. Virginia Muir challenged me to put the outline into words at a time I felt inadequate. Floyd Thatcher's affirmation made me *feel* like a writer. Mary Ruth Howes, with her perception and editorial skill, has helped me to see and clarify the rough spots in the manuscript.

For people . . . I give thanks!

Janice W. Hearn

Contents

PART I
WANDERINGS IN BITTERNESS

1. The Bitterness of My Soul 13
2. *This* Is Joyous Living? 21
3. How Do I Live with This Commitment? . . . 27

PART II
ROADWAYS TO PEACE

4. Love: The Fence Comes Down 37
5. Joy: Enjoy Yourself 48
6. Peace: A Bridge over Troubled Waters . . . 58
7. Patience: Establish Your Heart 68
8. Kindness: Let Kindness Be My Rule 79
9. Generosity: Pass It On 88
10. Fidelity (Commitment): A Sense of Belonging . 98
11. Adaptability: Who, Me . . . Change? . . . 108
12. Self-Control: Freedom to Decide 119

9

PART I

WANDERINGS IN BITTERNESS

*I wander to and fro all my life long
in the bitterness of my soul.
Yet, O Lord, my soul shall live with thee;
do thou give my spirit rest.
Restore me and give me life.*

Isaiah 38:15–16, NEB

1

The Bitterness of my Soul

SLOWLY I COULD SEE myself becoming the kind of person I most hated to be: hardened, cynical and hopeless. Sometimes I stood by the kitchen sink thinking I might flip out. I must be going crazy, I told myself, as I just stood there trying to gain self-control.

The kitchen sink was my frustration place—I spent a lot of time at it. Though I could not understand or verbalize what was wrong with me, I could feel. I would just stand, shaking, as restlessness and frustration swept over me, choking me. Life seemed too difficult to live, and there were times when I wished I did not have to bother. But my babies needed me. I could not leave them. There was no answer . . . was there? I was trapped by life, lousy life.

On the surface, it looked as if I had everything going for me. I sailed through school with nearly all A's. During college I managed to work for room and board, and also earned my tuition through scholarships and by working in the laboratory of the hospital. I was active in many organizations and won several awards—awards for being outstanding this or outstanding that. But though others may have believed me outstanding, to myself I never quite measured up.

People told me I was pretty. I didn't believe them. I thought they were putting me on and let their comments run off my back, even when I was selected for the May Day Court.

I married the young man who was considered the prime catch in the little community where I grew up. I trained for my registry as a medical technologist, and passed the test with flying colors. My babies were born healthy and whole, a boy followed by two girls.

All my life, I had the material things I needed, and most of what I wanted. Sometimes this meant working for it, but I can only think of two things I have wanted and not had: a tree house as a child, and a piano as an adult. I haven't given up yet on the piano.

Why, then, was I unhappy? It is only as I look back that I can begin to understand. Life did not turn out the way I expected. All my romantic ideas of marriage and babies went down the drain with the six years of diaper washwater. Where was the happiness I dreamed of, longed for, and expected? I was bone tired, and disappointed. I felt like a robot, a slave to my family and home.

Some of my discontent was the result of unrealistic expectations from marriage. Always an avid reader, I devoured hundreds of romantic novels during my teenage years. These and the few movies I saw, always gushy in those days, gave me an exaggerated portrait of marital bliss.

I approached marriage anticipating a fairytale. I envisioned afternoon picnics on a hillside, long walks holding hands, evenings before the fireside reading Shakespeare, trips to the theater. Instead, I found myself working fourteen to sixteen hours a day, resenting my husband's forty-hour work week, too worn out to hold hands or pack picnics, no energy for Shakespeare, and very little money for the theater.

I walked into this disenchantment straight out of college where I had excelled in everything. There I could measure my results in the tangible: the honoraries, the clubs, the awards, and finally, the *summa cum laude*. Now, I was faced with almost no recognition for what I was doing. Neal, who leans toward quietness and objectivity, could see no reason for lavishing praise. Why should he praise me for doing only what was my job?

I began to feel that I was worthless. I was caught in the conflict of wanting with all my heart to be a wife and mother —but not able to visualize results or even to keep up with the mountainous workload. I felt unfulfilled. I hated not being noticed for anything I'd done.

No one understood me, I thought. Other persons did not have problems, I told myself. Only me. I had been cheated.

Inability to communicate my true feelings led to repression. Actually, it was impossible for me to say then what my true feelings were, let alone express what I did feel. My emotions were vague and unarticulated. I felt irritable, crabby, jittery, nervous, afraid of other people, and confused. I didn't understand why I felt the way I did, and that caused me further conflict. As I saw it then, my crankiness and anxiety were sure symptoms of mental instability. I had long prided myself on being mentally stable, and here I

was, acting like a nut. I was fearful of losing my sanity, and
would not have believed anyone who told me I was simply
angry.

I don't know how long I'd been angry. Maybe always.
Sometimes I think I was born a spunky little fighter. Yet I
learned to deny that part of me—anger was bad or wrong.
In the era in which I grew up, children were still taught to
be seen and not heard. More unacceptable than being heard
was expressing anger. Nice people, and nice ladies in particular, did not act that way. I think I actually believed that
I was abnormal if I felt anger.

Only in a few instances do I remember feeling emotion as
a child. The time or two when I felt and dared to express
anger, it was squelched.

For example, one snowy morning on the way to school, I
had a vicious fight with an older, and bigger, girl. She had
run into the back of my sister's new bicycle, causing Marge
to fall. The teacher called us inside before school began, and
talked to us about fighting. All the while she talked I sat
there at my desk, tearing up all my papers and throwing
the pieces around the room. I don't recall the detail of the
teacher's words—only that I felt guilty for years because I
had allowed myself to be angry and show it.

Thus, I learned to hold my negative feelings to myself.
This became largely an unconscious habit, although at times
it was nearly conscious. I could not have identified what I
was doing as repression. But I was sometimes aware of hiding
or trying to deny my feelings. It was a strange mixture of
knowing and not knowing.

My habit of repression was continued and refined after
marriage. I learned early that Neal did not like me to raise

my voice or to grumble. Besides, I had seen enough of unhappy marriages in some of the people around me that I
was determined to have a good one, even if I had to lie to
myself. A good one meant the fairytale kind, of course. I felt
I was responsible to keep the peace. When I felt resentful
because he watched TV while I washed dishes and babies, I
held it to myself. I harbored and nurtured the real and
imagined slights until I carried within myself a huge hunk
of hatred and hostility, cold as an iceberg.

Like an iceberg, part of it surfaced now and then. When I
tried to communicate to Neal how I felt, I could only cry.
Because I could not accept angry feelings as normal and
identify them, I could not express to him that I was angry.
So I cried. And he shouted that he couldn't figure out what
had happened or what was wrong with me. So I pushed it all
back down for a while longer.

But I was beginning to find out that repression didn't
work. My negative feelings came out in ways I didn't expect,
or even understand. I became a chronic complainer. I was a
negative and cynical person, and I hated myself every time
I said something I had to regret later. I criticized others and
put them down when they did not meet my expectations.
Then I felt guilty for days afterward because I had said
something behind someone's back, or had inadvertently made
a statement with a double meaning right to their face.

Because my mind could not handle my repressed feelings,
it pushed them onto my body. My body responded by catch-
ing every cold and flu bug which passed through town. For
two years I was tormented by recurring bladder infections. I
nearly lived on antibiotics. Perhaps for a week or two I
would be off the medication—once for only two days—but

then I'd go scurrying back to the doctor doubled over with pain and fever. I knew only that I was sick, and it was destroying my life's energy.

Some nights, usually after a disagreement with Neal, I would lie in bed sobbing hysterically. Since that kept him awake, I'd often go to the bathroom and close the door until I could cry quietly. Then I'd go back to bed and cry myself to sleep, waking up with a soggy pillow and red, swollen eyes. Those mornings I knew I needed some kind of help. Often I picked up the phone and dialed the church number, only to hang up before it could ring. My fear of telling another person my problems was greater than my despair. I forced myself back into the routine of the day, and sometimes almost forgot my tearful night—until the next one occurred.

Other nights I was plagued by fear. I'd wake up, certain I'd heard a noise, or that someone was in the house. I worried constantly that someone would hurt the children. My imagined fears were compounded by real terror one night when a carload of teenagers drove up our driveway and across the lawn, narrowly missing the corner of the room where Steve slept. I was more frantic after that. Add to this the fact that I saw tornado clouds in every thunderstorm, and it gives you the idea. I was a bundle of nerves at night. I'd lie awake for hours, listening. When Neal wasn't home, I slept with the lights on. For a time, I would not go to bed until I'd looked under it and behind the doors to insure that no one was hidden. I rarely slept through an entire night.

Nothing gave me satisfaction. When I found a new activity, one in which I thought I might be happy, restlessness would overtake me. The search for contentment drove me on continuously and relentlessly. I went back to work part time.

I began to train my dog for obedience work. I made draperies for the house. I went to meetings. I landscaped the backyard. I threw parties, and they were fun—but the fun didn't last. Most of my friends moved away from the town where we lived, and I felt left behind, lost.

Then our daughter Diane fell and injured her neck, and I was filled with guilt because I was not home when it happened. She would not have been hurt, I felt certain, if I had not been out working. Shortly afterward, our other daughter Sharon needed surgery to close a blood vessel in her head, and complications put her in and out of the hospital for most of a month. Then, during the summer which followed, the kids had several small accidents that required emergency room trips. These things increased my feeling of agitation.

Going to church didn't help. Our pastor was a gifted speaker, and I was greatly inspired by his sermons. I went home determined to be a better mother, but before I had the kids' clothes hung up, I was shaking all over, trying not to yell. During those days I was also attempting to stop smoking, because I knew it was harmful. I would sit in church, listening to the sermon and feeling guilty, and resolve to go home and quit, cold turkey. But only when my husband bribed me with a trip to the Caribbean if I would stop for two years was I able to give up cigarettes.

Church didn't work for me because it evoked too much guilt. The churches in which I grew up externalized Christianity. As long as you did not wear lipstick, play cards, dance, drink or smoke, and such, you were in. Once when I was twelve and had my hair cut short, a church member told me that men were going to "get upset" looking at my bare neck . . . I should wear my hair long.

Some of the meanest people I have ever known called

themselves Christians. It seemed to me that to be a Christian meant to put on a sour face and exit from the world, never again to enjoy being alive. Very vividly, I remember in junior high school listening to an older girl give a testimony in church. She wore no makeup, her dress was dark and unstylish, and her hair was rolled up on one of those rat things. During the altar call that evening, I prayed: "When I am an old woman [this meant about twenty to me then], Jesus, I won't mind being ugly. *Then*, I'll be a Christian. I promise."

So, the church as I had seen it did not have any answers for me. It only pointed up my shortcomings and my failures and placed demands on me which I could not meet. It increased my conflict because it made me try to change myself; and when I failed, I hated myself more.

Then my husband had a job offer in San Diego. We moved, and for a while life was exciting. Caught up by adventure, I think I believed I had left my worries behind me. It was fun to drive across the country, stay in motels, and look for a new home. I was distracted from my problems. Painting and decorating the new house kept me involved for months, and a temporary calm settled over my life.

But not for long. Soon I had painted, planted, pruned, and sewn myself into total exhaustion again. Children were everywhere. Groups of fifteen and twenty would swoop through the house; some even brought their lunches and stayed all day. Car pools, houseguests, the state test for my profession, my new job—all drove me to distraction. Less than a year after we moved, once more I found myself at the kitchen sink—a new sink, the same old problem—feeling the choking sensation of frustration engulfing me, and wondering, once again, if I were going crazy.

2

This *Is Joyous Living?*

By this time I had begun to suspect something was unique in the new church we had joined. We chose it for our usual reasons: it was large; the pastor was a wonderful speaker; but primarily because it has a pipe organ, which my husband loves.

I managed to get through the membership class and the examination by the church session without being affected very much. The Sunday we joined, I nearly bolted out the door when the pastor shook my hand, and said, "Jan, we have a task for you." But the warmth of the welcome, with the congregation swarming about us, charmed me. It said to me what I longed to hear: there *is* something to this church business!

I joined a young women's circle, and began to say to myself after meetings, "There *is* something different here. But what is it?" As I listened to the pastor speak, I saw he was not sour-faced and stern like the "Christians" of my child-

hood. Instead, he seemed to be downright joyous. What did
he have? Then I began to notice his wife, who was friendly,
warm, and smiling.

When a Faith/at/Work Conference was announced and
described as a way to make your faith more real, I was curi-
ous enough that I planned to attend with a friend. All the
while I was still muttering to myself that something was
different about this church.

When the evening of the conference arrived, I was scared
silly. I hoped my babysitter would not be home. She wasn't.
My friend went on without me. Minutes later, the sitter's
parents dropped her off at my door, with apologies for her
lateness. I didn't know whether to thank them or hit them,
but driven by curiosity, I went on to the conference. When I
arrived they were singing: "Seek and ye shall find, knock
and the door will open. . . ."

Captivated by the words of the song, yet more afraid and
lonely than I've ever been in my life, I sneaked into the back
row. Always terrified of large groups, I felt conspicuous and
out of place and wished for a corner where I could hide.
This was my invariable reaction to groups. Uncertain of
my own worth, I tended to react much the same way with
individuals, particularly if I did not know them. Introductions and getting acquainted were sheer agony. I felt al-
ternately dumb, guilty, or feared being a burden. Sometimes
I felt all three at once. Most of the time when I was with
other people, I wanted to fold up like a flower at the end
of day.

But I wasn't allowed to stay in the security of the back
row for very long. After a few people spoke of their experiences with Christ, we were told to break into groups of four

persons—with people we did not know. Suddenly I found myself in a group with the pastor, Louis Evans, Jr., and I was terrified. *Now* he would discover who I really was, and I would rather not have him know.

As the evening went by we played group games. In one, we were to decide what kind of animal the others resembled. The group all agreed: I was a rabbit, cowering and shaking, and they only wanted to pet me. Lou's personal warmth came through to me, and I could say to him that I wanted to discover for myself what he had. When he took my hand, I felt a surge of power, as if something came from him to me. For the first time in my life, I prayed aloud. My simple, embarrassed, unaddressed prayer was something like this: "Help us to find what we're looking for."

Before we went home that evening, the four in our group committed ourselves to be brothers and sisters. I did not know what commitment meant, but it sounded like a good idea. I have not kept up with the other persons from that group. But Lou became the big brother I had longed for when I was growing up.

The next day of the conference was similar, with small groups taking much of the time. In one group, a man said to me: "You're angry, aren't you?"

"Why, yes, I am!" I replied. I hadn't realized until that day just how horribly angry and frustrated I was with what life had given me.

Opening up, baring one's emotions for the first time is exhausting. I left the conference early, and stopped on the way home for a pizza to take out, so I wouldn't have to cook. As I was putting out plates my husband said something, and I turned around, ready to really let him have it. It was an unusual response for me, because I normally repressed my anger. Recognizing my angry feelings that afternoon must have freed me to *be* angry.

But I did not let him have it. I felt Christ beside me as surely as if he had tapped me on the shoulder, and he seemed to say: "Is this the kind of love you have seen this weekend?"

So . . . this was what was different! *God was real!* He did not just sit there in the clouds and look down at me. He was not an old man with a beard. He spoke to me in a way that made me understand that he would live with me, if I wanted him.

The week following was a struggle. Now that I had found the difference, I didn't know if I wanted it! Jesus Christ followed me around the house, everywhere I went. I could not shake him. He would not go away. I knew he would give me no rest until I decided one way or the other what I was going to do about him.

Once again, I found myself dialing the phone and hanging up before it rang. I wanted to ask Lou to help me with what was going on, but my fear of being a burden won out over my desire for help. Deep inside, also, I knew it was something I alone must solve. Finally, in desperation, as I was pushing the vacuum cleaner one day, I thought: *OK, Jesus, I'll do it. You can have my life.* Still I felt him pushing me, asking me to go beyond to something more. Embarrassed beyond any description, I knew I had to kneel and pray out loud. It nearly killed me, but I knelt beside my bed and committed my life to him.

For weeks afterward, my feet did not touch the ground. My personal problems seemed to disappear. I knew only joy, and I felt like shouting from the rooftops. With tears running down my face, and more than a little afraid, I told my husband what had happened. Then I told a whole group of people in a Wednesday evening church class. All my life I had felt frightened and inferior in a group of people. That night I knew no fear as I told the class about God's becoming real to me and my joy. I did not even come back to earth when Lou told me to remember there might be some closets in my life to clean. (Later those words meant a lot to me.)

I expected the rest of my life to be gloriously happy. No more problems, I told myself. I've finally made it!

Gradually, though, I began to touch the ground again. Some of my old habits were returning. I felt critical toward others. Much of the time I was angry, hating both myself and other people. I yelled at my kids, and condemned myself in the next breath. I came home from my afternoon job, cooked dinner, and spent the evenings huddled in the corner of the sofa, exhausted. My babysitter quit, and I took the kids to a nursery. Then school started, and this year, for the first time, all three were to be in school. But there was a shortage of classrooms, and each child was going to school and coming home on a different schedule. I found myself emotionally strung out. The struggle to continue working under the strain of the children's schedule, coupled with my personal unrest, became impossible. Quitting my job gave me slight relief.

The reversal to my previous state left me totally confused. I had thought following Christ would be the answer to all my problems. I expected him to erase my troubles, to wipe them away with one magical swipe of his arm. Instead, I found myself more angry than before—or at least, I felt more angry, and recognized it as anger. What seemed worse, I could no longer hold the anger in with the effectiveness I once had. It slipped out more often. I found myself shaking uncontrollably at the least provocation—like spilled milk or scattered toys—and it seemed I had plenty of provocation. I felt mean, like a witch—horrible and ugly.

Much of my hostility was directed toward Neal. Unaware that I needed to look within myself for the cause of my unhappiness, I tried to blame him. He certainly had changed, hadn't he? He'd tricked me, I thought. Instead of the pleasant, outgoing man I'd married, he had grown quiet and every bit as serious as me. (I'd always considered myself too serious about life.) All these things I muttered to myself, but not to him. The anger festered into bitterness and hatred. Almost daily I considered divorce, but the thought of being alone was more frightening than being unhappy.

Nothing made sense. Here I was, a few months after my commitment, with problems which seemed worse than the ones with which I began. Didn't being born again mean I was a new person? Didn't having Christ in me through his Holy Spirit mean I would be joyful and victorious? How was I to relate love and joy and peace to my *real* life which was filled to the brim with problems?

3

How Do I Live
with This Commitment?

As I LOOK BACK, I see that I had three choices in responding to my confusion. I could have thrown out the whole business of the Christian life. There were times when I wanted to do just that. When I began to see that my old problems were still with me, often my tearful nights lengthened into tearful days. Once or twice I cried all night, got the kids and my husband out the door in the morning, cried all day, washed my eyes with cold water and shaped myself up for the evening, only to return to bed and cry myself to sleep again. Probably the only reason I did not give up my commitment was because deep down I knew it was the only chance I had, other than being crazy.

Choice two was the option to closet myself away from the world. I could have lived most of my hours away from the reality of life, and assumed a victorious attitude about the problems I could not change. I could have pretended to my Christian friends and said everything was beautiful. But

I could not pretend to myself. Escapism seemed little better than craziness. Besides, it honestly didn't work. I couldn't hide in the bedroom praying and reading my Bible when the kids were having a major knock-down-drag-out in the family room.

For a while I wanted to believe it would work like this. It would be an easy way to live—just let Jesus take away my problems. When, about eight months after my commitment to Christ, I was nearly immobilized by constant headaches, I prayed and hoped Christ would heal me instantly.

"Why not?" I used to shout at him. "If you can heal people who walk up on the stage to see a faith healer, why can't you heal me?" I had read an article which said that many people who were healed in that way had first doubted even the reality of God. "OK, God," I shouted, "if you can heal those who doubt, why won't you heal me when I believe so strongly?"

But that was not his answer for me. I nearly banged my aching head into the wall in my stubbornness before I was willing to accept what he was teaching me. Only after months of struggle and ceaseless pain would I learn *his* solution for my headaches.

So, only because choice one and choice two did not work, was I able to discover a third way, a way in which I can live life realistically and honestly as Christ's person. Throughout this process, I have been blessed by being in the kind of church community which has supported and loved me as I have discovered this new lifestyle. It has not been easy. Very few days have I danced joyously among the daisies. Many days I've struggled with depression. I fully expect it will take my entire lifetime to reach Christian maturity. Only when I am in heaven will I have reached the full potential God has given me.

It is only slowly, painfully, and often with great impatience that I have learned something of what the Christian life is about. Childhood church experiences had left me with the impression that once a person was converted that was it. Safe from hell was the only important thing. Now I began to understand that being a Christian meant much more.

First of all, I learned that the Incarnation is more than just a baby at Christmas—*it is the Holy Spirit living in me today.* Jesus himself told us this (John 14:16–23). I pored over Jesus' words, soaking them up. I cannot explain this concept in good theological language, but I understand it for myself—God the Father and Jesus Christ the Son live in me—have made their home with me—through the Holy Spirit.

Yes, this changes my eternal destination, but I believe the Holy Spirit was given to show me how to live now. He is a teacher, a counselor, a comforter. The Holy Spirit abides in me in order to help me follow Christ's way. And as he lives in me, he works from the inside out. It is not a matter of following certain rules, but an attitude of openness to his work in changing me. I have discovered that being born again does not mean I am instantly changed into a carbon copy of Christ. It doesn't even mean I am problem-free or perfect. Rather, it means my direction in life has been changed. I walk a new road, one which goes somewhere! I have begun a process, a purposeful life, and through it I am finding the satisfaction I've longed for all my life.

For a person who had expected *results*, the acceptance of *process* has sometimes been difficult. I've had to learn that

my expectations are often far from God's plans. Understanding some of the ways the Holy Spirit works has helped
me begin to relax and enjoy the process.

I began to discover how the Holy Spirit works early in my
Christian career. I made the decision to give my life to Christ
about five years ago, in the springtime. By late summer I
was experiencing the frustration of seeing that I was not so
new after all. I had been reading my Bible and anything
else about God I could put my hands on. One day I picked
up a book which talked about looking at life from the good
side, instead of focusing on one's problems. Now, this may be
great psychology for a healthy person, but it nearly ruined
me. It almost sent me into total despair because I was unable
to follow the suggestions.

In desperation, I turned to Coke Evans, our pastor's wife.
By this time I was beginning to understand what was meant
by commitment of other persons. I knew Coke and Lou were
in this with me, and I began to trust them enough to let them
know my problems. Coke suggested I see Lou for counseling.
While once I was afraid to turn to a pastor for help, now I
could barely wait to get there. It was a relief to have someone available. I poured out all the feelings I had been repressing for so many years. I wrote pages upon pages of
hatred and hostility. My stomach churned and tied itself in
knots, and I cried and wept. Lou's ears must still be burning
from some of the things I told him. Patiently, he listened.
As he listened he continued to love and accept me, even in
my ugliness.

I cannot think about those days even now without crying.
But now the tears are of joy and wonder for the kind of love
which could keep on loving me when I hated myself. Lou and
Coke and a group of women in a little prayer circle I was

attending all kept me going. Their love, support and understanding taught me much about the way God loves.

Through this, I began to see the guidance of the Holy Spirit. I realized Christ could not work further in my life until some of the garbage was out of the way. By garbage, I mean all the things which were wrong inside of me—the hate, hostility and bitterness I'd stored up and hoarded. Through the Holy Spirit's leading, I began to perceive that the negative feelings alone were not sinful or abnormal. Everyone is capable of anger. It was the piling up and holding them to myself which was sin—poisonous sin. As one of Edgar Lee Masters's ghosts in his *Spoon River Anthology* put it, while the tongue is sometimes an "unruly member— silence poisons the soul."

My harbored hostilities and bitterness had filled my life. It was like a perverse kind of love-affair, almost as if I cherished my hatred and resentment toward others. There was no room left for learning God's ways. For this reason, I saw that the Holy Spirit might lead me into a difficult situation, in order to help me get rid of the poison. He doesn't only give joy. He may take me through pain, but he will give me strength and the support of others while I am there. While I may not know his purpose, I am learning to trust his guidance, because I have seen the results on the other side of the tunnel.

I have learned that I have a choice whether or not I will have the Holy Spirit in my life; and also whether or not I'll follow him. Just as with any relationship, I have to desire and work toward intimacy. Knowing the Holy Spirit requires some effort on my part.

There was a time after my initial commitment when I decided to discover everything I could about the Holy Spirit.

I scurried about looking for books, reading everything the Bible says about him, asking my friends what they knew. The results were that while I knew a little more about him, I was still unsatisfied. My real answer came only through prayer, when I realized I could learn more only through the Spirit's own teaching. I need to know *him*, not *about* him. And so, I still read, study the Bible, talk to friends. But I learn to know him mostly by living with him. As I struggle to write about the Spirit, I realize how limited my knowledge is. With all I know, how much more I do not know!

Quietness seems to be a necessity. Once I went to a worship service where people were "waiting for the Spirit." It became a storytelling affair because everyone was afraid of silence. Perhaps we are all a bit afraid of quietness—or too busy to be quiet. But, only as I take time to be silent, can I know what he's teaching me, where he's leading me.

But how do I know if it's his leading, or my personal desire? Often I know because his answers come when I do not expect them: a flash insight during prayer or Bible study; awakening during the middle of the night; being inspired by a speaker. But the real test of the Spirit's guidance is whether the idea persists. Usually the thought will not leave me until I do something about it. Last week I read a story in the paper about a baby with a terminal illness. I could not shake the story from my mind until I wrote a note to the parents letting them know I would pray for them. Then I had peace.

The key to guidance is *obedience*. So far, God has not shown me my whole life laid out in black and white. Often I wish he would. But I admit that it would not be very challenging if I knew all the answers. As I obey what the Spirit tells me, he gives me the next step. If I hesitate, I stay right where I am. Until I take the first step, he will not give me a second. Once, in stubbornness, I refused to write a letter for fear of what the person would think of me. "He doesn't know me, God. He'll think I'm some kind of a nut." When three months later, I was still feeling the same nudgings, I finally wrote, though reluctantly. He didn't think I was a nut. He answered with a two-page letter full of ideas which have been invaluable to my writing. The result of even delayed obedience was direction.

Another thing I've learned about the Spirit's leading is to be *flexible*. For a long time I typed the church sermons. I believed it was one of my gifts. When I began to feel indications I should no longer be doing the sermons, and finally experienced a total loss of power, I became flustered. I didn't know if a gift could change. After balking, as usual, I called Lou, who knows a lot more about being a Christian than I do. He assured me gifts may change as time goes on, and one of the joys of the Christian life is flexibility—the willingness to follow wherever the Spirit is leading.

In the area of gifts of the Spirit, one of the most critical things I've discovered is not to ask for what I *want*. Instead, it's better to ask for what I need, or for something to bless the lives of those about me. Once when I was selfishly praying for a gift which I wanted, God gave it to me. But in addition, he gave me a different kind of gift which I needed. In my joy over getting what I wanted, I nearly missed seeing all he gave me. Now, as I look back, the gift I wanted means little to me, although it was helpful at that time. But I wouldn't trade in a million years the thing I needed: his forgiveness.

"The real proof of the Spirit-filled life is the fruit." That statement used to scare me. The first time I heard it, I was

dead certain I would never qualify. I didn't see much fruit
in my life. Then one day I realized the fruit can't grow until
the plant does.

I am not much of a gardener. My brown thumb is a standing family joke. Once when I planted tomato plants, they
were the same size at the end of the summer as when I
planted them. They were halfway up a hill, and I was not
interested enough to do more than give them an occasional
watering. But my father planted the rest of the flat, and by
midsummer, his well-watered, fertilized, and cared-for plants
were producing bushels of fruit.

I think the fruits of the Spirit in our lives are much like
this. The Spirit gives us the fruit freely. But there are
things in our distorted lives which prevent us from receiving the fruit. So, he has to do some groundwork first, caring
for us, pinching off the dead leaves, fertilizing us. During
this time we may not see the results. The roots on the plant
grow out of sight, underground. It takes a process of nur-
turing and time before the fruit grows on the plant. Likewise, I think the fruits of the Spirit come into our lives
slowly, sometimes painfully, but always beautiful to behold
when full-grown.

This process requires my cooperation and openness, however. He doesn't force his "improvements" on me. While he
has taken away my fear of groups of people and my fear of
night, the Holy Spirit—Christ in me—seems to work basically through a teaching and growing experience. In the
chapters which follow, I'd like to share what I am learning
about living as a Christian.

PART II

ROADWAYS
TO
PEACE

The Spirit . . . produces in human life
fruits such as these:
love, joy, peace,
patience, kindness, generosity,
fidelity, adaptability, and self-control.
Galatians 5:22–23, Phillips

4

Love: The Fence Comes Down

ONCE I WROTE in my diary: "I am afraid, scared stiff of love. I'm afraid to be loved and afraid to love. I'm terrified because I don't know what it will mean to me."

I don't know why I feared love so greatly. For a time I searched for causes. I learned that being hurt was one of the factors which caused me to draw back from loving or being loved. I recognize now, as an adult, that being hurt is part of any close relationship. But my child's mind did not understand that fact. Though I can't remember much about it, I must have been a very sensitive child, with fragile, easily wounded feelings.

I do recall a shopping excursion with an aunt whom I loved dearly. I was excited because shopping trips were a two-or-three-times-a-year happening. Besides, I had a quarter to spend! When the time came for me to look for something, my aunt asked where I wanted to shop. I chose the five-and-ten-cent store. My aunt mocked my words sarcasti-

cally to her friend, loud enough for me to hear. Today I
know she was probably tired and ready to go home and the
walk to another store was an unwelcome chore. But then, my
entire life was crushed. I loved the dollhouse swingset which
I purchased with my quarter. But, in the following years,
each time I looked at it the pain of the moment with my aunt
came back to me, and I stopped loving her.

How many other times I experienced this kind of pain, I
can only guess. If I could get more in touch with my little
girl feelings, I suspect I would find many other such hurts.
To my child's mind, anyone who loved me would not hurt me.
If they wounded me with cruel (to me) words, or thought-
less (to me) actions, it followed that they did not love me
at all.

I learned the tool of repression early enough that I did
not tell anyone when they hurt my feelings. I secretly in-
terpreted each incident as rejection of me. I wanted to cry
the day my aunt disappointed me. Instead, I held onto the
pain and harbored it. The only way I was able to deal with
it was to withhold my love and refuse to accept hers. It
meant, eventually, that I was holding back on loving anyone, or receiving love from just about anyone I had known
for longer than a day! I was afraid to take the risk of being
hurt again and ended up building an emotional chain link
fence around myself.

My search through my past helped me know more about
myself. But in the end the causes didn't matter. What
really mattered was that I felt unloved and unworthy. I had
to prove to everyone, but most of all to myself, that I had a
reason for living. I felt inferior, insecure, inadequate, never
able to measure up to others. Silently I said to each person
I met, "Pardon me for living." This made me defensive and

always ready to justify myself. To compensate, I became deeply competitive and perfectionistic. If I were perfect and excelled in everything, then no one would criticize me. I could even like myself a little because I had proved I could do almost everything better than anyone else I knew.

With such a large part of me closed off by the emotional chain link fence I'd built, I was unable to feel anyone loved me. I could have blamed other people for my state, or the churches which had allowed me to grow up not hearing of God's love. And for a while I did, until I understood blaming others could not change the way I was. But the Holy Spirit could.

I believe love is alive in me because of Christ's healing power which comes to me both directly from himself and through other people. I once thought I could not love, or that I had not been given the ability to love. Now I know love is a part of every human being. It was in me too, like a tiny seed, lying there all those years, dormant. When the Holy Spirit came into my life, the love seed was able to germinate and begin to grow. It hasn't been easy or magical; rather, it's been a slow and sometimes painful process.

It was not difficult for me to believe that God loves me, once I had made the commitment to Christ. My conversion experience was real enough for me to sense that if Christ was interested in the mess I had made of my life, he *had* to love me. I began to understand that the reason the church of my childhood had never made sense to me was that I had never met Christ there. I had only heard the negatives. When finally I saw Christ for who he is, I knew I was loved by God. It was as if some eternal truth was now embedded in my life.

Though God's love was no longer an issue with me, the

human situation still was. Even when others told me they loved me I didn't believe them. I wanted to make them prove it. Maybe they loved me only because they were Christians, or because God put it on them. But Christ had given me a church full of loving, patient people, and after a while I had to believe they meant it when they said they loved me. Through the years, I have begun to understand many things about love.

The first thing I learned was that I must want to be loved. I have to receive the love of others. For years I would not let other persons into my life to love me. I closed the doors because I did not believe myself lovable. Then I sat behind my self-built prison walls screaming, "No one loves me!" It all seems a little silly as I look back, but there was nothing funny about it then.

Even now, I sometimes catch myself letting affirmation run right off my back. A few months ago, I wrote an article for the church newsletter which many people liked. For weeks afterwards, people called me or walked up to me in church to tell me so. I thanked them, but later realized I was not really accepting their praise. The good thing about this experience was that I could see what I was doing and recognize the destructiveness of my actions. Then I asked the Lord to help me receive what others give me.

Part of my problem in receiving has been wanting other people to respond in a certain way. Yet in doing so, I have not given them a chance to love me in their own way, or worse, have not recognized the tokens of love they've given.

In a small way, I saw this with my children about a year ago. It was my birthday, and no one remembered. This was unusual for our family, I might add; it had never happened before. Well, the children were aghast when they discovered what had happened, and they decided to remedy the situation. They made cards, all addressed to "the best mommy in the world." Each gave me the gifts they felt I needed. Steve had heard me say I was broke, so he gave me a quarter. Diane gave me a handful of pennies and an old papier-mâché turtle which she'd made in school the year before, and which had made the rounds of the family on previous occasions. Sharon gave me an old stuffed rabbit to take to bed with me and a book so I could read myself a story before I went to sleep. It was the sweetest birthday I've ever had. But if I had awaited some specific or spectacular gift, I might have missed out on the best love gifts of all.

One of the most critical factors for me was learning to love myself. This came about through counseling, small groups, prayer circles and just plain friends. As I talked out my feelings about the past, all the repressed anger and hostilities fell away.

But the process was not as easy or as quiet as those words might indicate. It was rather violent when I first began to let the anger out. I went home and shouted at Neal, recalling the pain of a multitude of ways I'd been injured. I listed all the times I believed others had intentionally tried to hurt me. I didn't want to forgive anyone for anything.

Everything that was wrong with me I blamed on my parents. I wrote a venomous letter to my mother. I was very much like a rebellious teenager. I could plainly see how ugly I was inside, and I hated myself more.

But gradually as the bitterness and resentment, and even hatred, were let out, I softened a bit—and became more rational. With the weight of the hostility gone, I could look with clearer eyes on the past. I saw the good things my parents had given me, and was able to write and tell them what I appreciated—characteristics such as responsibility and honesty they'd taught me, the good health they'd nurtured, and so forth. I began to see that regardless of how I had felt in the past, I did not have to go on in the same way. This was a new time, and my bucket was full of the love of other people. I started to like myself and appreciate the good things about me.

Most of the time now, I feel loved by others. I no longer have to seek the reassurance which I once needed. Many of the friends I treasure most have never said in words that they love me, but I know they do. I see it by the way they act, or by the smile on their faces.

Those people can even tell me something bad about myself and I can accept it. One friend whom I seldom see, but whose face lights up when I walk into the room, told me once on the telephone that I was acting paranoid. And I was. I was very upset that evening, and totally overreacting to a small incident. I could say to him, yes, you're right. For me, it was a high sign of my growth. For the first time in my life, I had been able to accept criticism without feeling unloved.

If the Holy Spirit had never done anything more than to give me this knowledge that I am loved, it alone would be a witness to his power.

But it has not stopped there. Loving myself and knowing others love me, too, has given me the desire to love other people. "Love your neighbor as yourself" means to me that I must be secure within before I can give love.

Probably the most difficult thing I have had to learn about loving another person is that love is not emotional dependence or possessiveness. For a time, I was so dependent upon two or three other people I could not function or make a decision without calling one of them to see what they thought about it. I was also very possessive toward these people. They belonged to me, I felt, and I was filled with jealousy every time they even spoke to others. I wanted to be special to them, to own them. Only as I began to develop self-worth could I separate myself emotionally from them. Our relationships have developed into two-way affairs, with interdependence on one another. As I was able to stop clutching them to myself, they were free to be themselves and to let me know of their need for me.

One very important discovery I've made is that love is making a commitment to stick around even when the going is rough. When I am hurt by someone, whether it is a real or imagined injury, my first impulse is still to flee the relationship. Christ has shown me that relationships can go on in spite of conflict and become even more meaningful, if I am willing to face knowing the painful part, as well as the delightful part, of relating to another person.

Recently, when a friend and I found a conflict in our relationship, we were able to talk about it. I felt she was trying to protect me, and she felt she was simply being helpful. I don't think either of us liked the other very much at that point, but because we are both Christians and love each other, our relationship survived. Not only that, we care more deeply about each other since then.

I don't believe, though, that we should go about confronting people at every turn of the road. I think it should be done only after prayerful consideration. If my feelings are such that I believe the relationship will not be damaged or destroyed, I probably would speak to my friend, with the intention of reconciliation. Other times, when I did not feel the relationship sturdy enough, I guess I would just talk to Christ about it. Sometimes I can be reconciled within myself and do not have to confront the other person.

Perhaps the most surprising thing I've learned is that the Christian thing to do may not always look to be the most loving. The loving way may even look unchristian to someone who doesn't understand the situation. Again, I believe strongly in the necessity of prayer here. In a problem situation which has existed over a period of time, I feel I must prayerfully decide how to act in a way which will be loving on a long-term basis.

We once had houseguests who stayed way beyond their welcome. I think if I could have seen the long-term result, I would have communicated my feelings. Instead, I sat around smiling like a Cheshire cat, while on the inside I smoldered. The resentments which grew out of the situation nearly ruined the friendship. If I could have spoken my feelings in a loving way, the relationship probably would not have been so severely damaged.

As I learn more about loving God's way, I see that love is not always the way I feel. It's easy to love when I feel warmth, tenderness, and compassion for another person. And it's easy to feel this way about a warm, loving person whom I enjoy and respect. I think I tend to be a responder as far as feelings go—I give back feelings. But I have difficulty feeling for everyone, and sometimes my emotions are inconsistent. For a time, this caused me great concern and a lot of guilt. Then I realized that it's pretty tough to feel much for a cold, distant person. I began to understand that love is the way I act. I can make a person feel loved and give him what he needs whether or not I am full of emotion about him. I think when Christ told us to love everyone we meet, he meant an attitude of kindness and compassion, and not a goopy feeling. Acting in a loving way regardless of feelings takes practice. It arises out of a discipline of listening to the proddings of the Holy Spirit, and then following them. It means making a decision of the will. William Barclay, in his *Letter to the Galatians and Ephesians* (p. 55, Daily Study Bible Series), states that love is a "deliberate effort."

I believe this is why habits and snap judgments become more loving as time goes on. The Holy Spirit has the power to come into my life and change my habits immediately. But could I handle it, psychologically, if he did? I don't think so. Neither would I place much value on something which came so easily. I think he has taught me how to handle life by the way he has worked in me. In teaching me to love and be loved, he has prepared me for the future. This may seem the most difficult way for me. But he gives me the power to live his way, the nudgings which help me see my mistakes, and the chance to try again. He has given me freedom and calls me constantly to be responsible to it. I respect a God who works like that.

I perceive a definite pattern in this process of learning to love other persons. First, I must recognize my hatred . . . or my apathy, because apathy is as much the opposite of love as hatred is. As I read my Bible, pray, and watch my interactions with other people, I constantly become more aware of the situations where I am unloving.

But I must go beyond recognition, and tell someone else. Always this is God. To verbalize my lack of love helps me to understand it. Sometimes I talk with another person about it.

As I begin to pray about my situation, and to understand

it, usually I want to change. Then I feel the willingness to let God change me, and work through me . . . and I begin to see positive results.

Sometimes I find these results painful. But once I've gone through them and can look back, I often find them rather amusing. I see the Holy Spirit putting me into the very place where I'd least like to be. I think he must have a wonderful sense of humor!

For example, one Sunday, just after I had become a Christian, I was sitting in the church pew before the service, praying that I could love the people I hated. Who should walk in and sit beside me in the pew, but a girl I really disliked! I couldn't believe it.

Peg and I had lived beside each other in the motel when our families moved to San Diego at the same time. I'm not sure why we found each other so disgusting, but the feeling was mutual. And then when we joined the same church I was angry to think I would have to face her. But the love of God brought us face to face that Sunday morning. We chatted after service, and a week or so later ended up in a small group situation during a circle meeting. We talked out our feelings, and left embracing each other. To this day we are still good friends. God's reconciliation lasts.

A similar experience helped me face a conflict in our church. I was angry and hateful toward those persons I knew had caused the tension. I felt very protective toward my church and the people who were being hurt by this disruption. For weeks I stewed. Then a friend noticed my unrest. She sat with me and listened. As I talked with her, I saw the ugliness of the way I felt and admitted it to her and to Christ. During the week which followed, I began to see tension as a by-product of growth, and discovered that I was not responsible to try to stop it, but to go on loving through it.

In several other situations I have experienced the same thing. The Holy Spirit keeps taking me back to face the persons and situations I dislike or reject. He teaches me to love those persons and to love through trying situations.

A few years ago I arrived fresh and enthusiastic at a conference, only to discover that the people there were very different from me. Some of them even reminded me of Christians I had known as a child—and I still rejected people like that. Now, here I was right in the middle of them for several days. Yikes! Everywhere I looked I saw and heard the external signs of Christianity—in the way they dressed, in their use of what I called "churchy" language. Well, I didn't sleep much at the conference, because I was struggling so with being put back into the kind of Christianity I had rejected. While others slept, I wrote and prayed . . . in the bathroom, because there was no other private place. You guessed it, by the end of the week I was able to see the beauty in those people. I could let them differ with me theologically, and keep my mouth shut about it. By the time I went home, I had actually grown to love some of them. This experience taught me not to categorize people, and to appreciate the diversity of the Body of Christ.

Love comes first on the list of the fruit of the Spirit, and I don't think it's there by accident. I believe it's God's plan for love to be in the same position in our lives. While I'm sure my family and friends can tell you how much I haven't learned about loving, I know I've begun the process through knowing Christ and his people. It seems a miracle that I no longer have to be afraid of love.

5

Joy: Enjoy Yourself

"WHAT'S HAPPENED to you since I saw you last?" my friend Gretchen asked me one day at prayer circle after a summer away. "You look happy . . . and beautiful!"

Since I tended to think of myself as being quite a failure when it came to being joyous, Gretchen's question surprised me. But she told me about the first time she had seen me and how confused I had appeared to her. Now several months had passed during which Christ had changed many things in my life, and when she saw me this time, something was different.

Gretchen's comments were taken up by the entire prayer group. I felt embarrassed by the attention but delighted with what they saw: "Yes, you are prettier." "Your face has lost the hard look—you're softer looking." "You seem joyful now."

This experience helped me to understand that being joyous is not always being a laughing or giddy person. Rather,

I think it is more often a quiet confidence which underlies our lives. The Greek word *chara* is used in the New Testament of a joy whose basis is God. I like that. To me it speaks of something deep-rooted and consuming which grows in our lives as the Holy Spirit lives in us.

At one time I understood joy as being only a very intense state of emotion. My conversion experience left me that way for weeks, and oh, it was fun! I was a very gay person, full of enthusiasm and energy.

Two or three times since then I have known the same kind of intense feeling during "mountaintop" experiences. For me there has been such closeness to God in these times that my feet have not even touched the ground. Once, during an intense prayer experience, I felt intertwined with God. I was rapturous, and wanted the feeling to last. Of course it didn't.

I've learned that this is only one kind of joy. While it is beautiful, it is escapist of me to want only that. Perhaps it is a promise of my potential for the future. Maybe that's what heaven is like. But I don't think I could handle living on such a high emotional plane all the time, right now.

These "wildly" joyous times for me seem like a child's day alone with mom. When I'm alone with one of my children, that child and I really get to know one another better. It is almost as if God takes me aside occasionally for a day alone with him. While it's special and a time to treasure, it isn't all there is to Christian life. I would not want to miss out on the quiet, deep-rooted joy I've found growing in me on a daily basis.

I believe this confident kind of joy comes about as a result of wholeness in living. God wants my mind as well as my emotion. I can praise him with bursting emotions, but I can also praise him by giving him my mind, my personality and my body. By this I mean that I need to let him into all aspects of my life. It isn't easy to do, and I'm not saying I do it well. But I see it as one of my goals in Christ.

Sometimes I focus on the emotional, like the mountain-top experience. Or, I spend time getting in touch with who I am, my personality, by exploring my feelings, learning to understand them, and allowing Christ to show me how to deal with them. Other times I get involved in a brain-busting class or a deeply intellectual book, and I struggle with all that I am to understand and grasp new (for me) concepts about God and life. Another day, another week, I find myself concentrating on my body: thinking about physical health, diet and exercise, and working to bring my decisions for discipline in this area into my daily life.

The "trick" is to not get stuck in any one area. When my friend Coke used to listen to me become overly excited about any one thing, she would gently tell me not to "major in it."

Because I am limited with my humanity, I can basically see only one area at a time. I need to live there for then, but be ready to move on when Christ decides. In this way, he teaches me that all of life belongs to God. When I respond to him with all that I am, I find a new kind of life-balance.

Life-balance comes from integrating the mind, emotion, personality and body. Spiritual well-being includes them all. One of the things resurrection brings about is this kind of integration. To me resurrection means not only that I will have eternal life. It means I have a new ability to live life in all its fullness and reality here and now. Christ came to tell us not to sit back and frown but to get out there and live.

To live in wholeness, enjoying life, has for me been simply to have a singleness of purpose. That may sound paradoxical. But I've found that as I keep Jesus Christ at the center of my life as the single most important focus of my days, the rest of life falls into place. While it sounds a simple task to keep Christ at the center, I often find it difficult. Again and again I wander away, and I have to keep coming back.

One of the things which most often causes me to lose my focus is my busyness. Normally I don't do something if I don't think it is really important. But I continually over-schedule myself, and end up living a hectic existence. I run from one place to the next with barely time to breathe. Even the dogs begin to eye me quizzically as I pop in and out of the house. I neglect my Bible study and prayer time, and start trying to be a do-it-yourself Christian, relying on my own power instead of God's.

At a time like this it helps me to look at things from the viewpoint of eternity. Then I can begin to establish priorities. How important is my tennis game or the meeting I have to attend, in view of eternity? Would it make a difference if I were not here today? When Jesus has first priority, the other things get done anyway, and a lot more smoothly than if I did them alone.

I experienced this not long ago when I attended a writer's conference held at a beautiful place called Mount Hermon, near Santa Cruz, California. Rustic buildings are surrounded by tall redwoods, and the dogwoods were blooming that week. In the woods, I rediscovered trilliums, wildflowers I had not seen since tramping through the woods with my father as a child. It was a quieting experience just to be there.

But as I went to classes and workshops and the Bible study during the week, I became very aware of the unquietness and misarrangement of my life. Everything I heard

seemed to speak to me personally, and when I left I knew
once again that Christ comes first. Nothing I can do or accomplish, through my writing or in any other area of my
life, means anything unless Christ is in the center position.
When he is the purpose for my living, I truly begin to live
in wholeness, health and quiet joy.

Still, there are days when I don't feel joyous, or even
good. Sometimes I feel lousy. Then it helps me if I assume
an attitude of joy toward life. It doesn't always solve my
problem, but if I can make a conscious decision about what
my attitude will be, it does usually soften the bad days.

To help me assume this attitude of joy in life, I try to
engage in creative activities or learning experiences. When
God created us in his own image, I think he filled us with
an urge to create and to learn. I know it helps me to be
happy when I'm doing something as simple as baking cookies
or attending a class.

Being aware of the beauty around me also increases my
joy. As I drive down the road, sometimes I am overwhelmed
by the intense blue of the sky or the sparkling effect of the
sunshine. I love to go to the beach and sit or walk, just enjoying being there. It quiets me on a day I feel grumpy and
restless, and on good days fills me with rejoicing for the
goodness of the Lord. It seems to me God gave us a beautiful
world not only to enjoy when we feel good, but to soothe us
when we are troubled.

Children seem to find joy in simple things. Maybe there's
a lesson for us there. They can even make pleasure out of a
disastrous situation, as I discovered a few months ago.

My neighbor had driven me in her station wagon to pick
up a new canopy bed for Diane. As Becky backed her car
into our driveway, she hit the concrete block wall, leaving

a pile of broken rocks and a bashed-up car. I was very upset, because she had been trying to help me when this terrible thing happened—somehow it injured my pride. All I could think of was the dollar bills it would take to fix her car. My children and hers, however, saw the fun of having a broken wall to put together. They carefully put all the pieces back, and covered it with a blanket until Daddy could get home. They took delight in what to us adults was an unpleasant situation.

Perhaps one of the nicest things I've experienced in being a Christian is a feeling of contentment about where I am in life. Age doesn't seem to matter as it once did. A doctor once said to my daughter: "Well, Sharon, here you are wanting to grow up, and your mother and I only want to go backwards." I quickly told him *he* might want to go backwards, but I don't. I don't think he believed me, but I meant it. I like it where I am. I've seen this in other Christian friends, too. One friend in her seventies I think of as a swinging grandmother. Her faith has given her a youth of spirit which wipes away any generation gap she encounters.

The most important step toward joyous living for me has been learning to accept myself. I used to think I could only accept myself if I were perfect. My house had to be spotless, and when I had guests I worked for days getting ready. Often I missed the fun of the occasion because I was worn out preparing for it. It was as if people visited me to see what I could do rather than to enjoy being with me. This put a huge burden on me, because I lived constantly for "what people would think."

Self-acceptance has not come easily, but only through a period of great struggle. Many things helped me as I progressed. One was a statement our pastor made, that it's just as selfish to hate yourself as it is to be superior. That hit home to me when I thought about how wrapped up I could become in putting myself down. I was continually focusing on the negative about myself, even to the point of ruining the good I had done. I recovered a sofa for a friend once, and it turned out beautifully. Even I was pleased, and she was delighted. But I was so unsure about my talents at that time that I worried for weeks about my work on the sofa. I actually dreamed that it fell apart!

A breakthrough came for me at a Faith/at/Work conference. Ralph Osborne reminded us that we are God's creation, and it is blaspheming God to hate his creation. Those words helped change my life. When I realized what it meant to be God's child, his creation, I had to reevaluate my position. While I still slip back occasionally into my favorite sin of putting myself down, I claim that thought again for myself, and proceed in a new way.

Another terribly difficult area of self-acceptance for me has been to admit I had weaknesses, because I wanted to be a perfect person. (How I could belittle myself, and still not acknowledge my real weaknesses, I haven't quite figured out.) Once I did admit my weaknesses and my problems to other people, however, I went to the other extreme and became caught up in them. There is a great deal of attention to be gained by always having a sad story to tell. In small groups, I wanted, for a time, to be the center of attention, rather than functioning as a part of the total group. I felt very sorry for myself in those days while I lived only in my problems. Then one day I realized what I was doing, and decided to change.

But as time went on, my efforts to change swung me in the other direction. Somehow I acquired the idea that to be a "successful" Christian I had to be victorious over all my problems, and that maturity meant to live smoothly without being ruffled about anything. I wanted to be self-sufficient, which is just about as bad as trying to be perfect or dwelling on problems. So I tried to act as if I had no problems. Pride, as well as fear of being a burden, made me shy away from letting other people know the real me. But that didn't work, and I began to see that I needed others. When I can admit my weakness to others, not in a sense of dwelling on it, but in a willingness to change, amazing things often happen. It seems that God begins to work and heal when there is an atmosphere which allows this kind of confession to other persons.

At one point after I had begun to be more open, I was corresponding with a friend who had seen only the successful side of my life. I was struggling with some particular problem, though I can't recall now what it was, and I told her about it in a letter. It was the beginning of a deep friendship. While once we were casual acquaintances, we now share long, intimate letters about our Christian growth. My sin of self-sufficiency had blocked our relationship. When I could stop hiding the real me from her, she felt comfortable letting me know her, too.

All this has caused me to adopt a new concept of Christian maturity. I now believe maturity means the ability to live day by day with myself, admitting who I am, liking myself, aware of my feelings and neither denying or repressing them. When I acknowledge them as they occur, I can work through them and grow. And as I share with others in this process, the Holy Spirit produces results beyond anything we could expect.

The ability to accept myself has given me new freedom in

life. I can recognize the good things about me and enjoy them. I can look at the not-so-good, and realize that is where I am, and in God's time the bad habits and qualities have potential for good. I no longer have to worry about what people think. While I still like my house to be clean, I don't drive myself to keep up with the clutter caused by three children and a houseful of pets. I can enjoy my guests, because I know they come to see me, and I don't have to worry about whether or not I have enough forks or the right kind of china. Likewise, I have more personal freedom. For example, once my sandal broke during a meeting of the cub scout pack. I was a den mother, too. While this would have given me fits at one time, now I was able to carry my shoes and leave barefoot—in the middle of November—laughing about it.

Self-acceptance has also given me a new attitude about other people. What I think of my own mental health, I tend to extend to others. When I was afraid that I might be a little nutty, I used to go around looking at other persons, wondering about them, too.

That this seems to be a universal habit was illustrated for me in a small group of women I belonged to. As the eight of us talked around the circle, we discovered that each had felt judged as inadequate by others at times; we had also all judged others' personal and mental abilities. We decided the predominant reason for this was our own insecurity. When we are unsure of ourselves, we are afraid what others will think, and we feel they are judging us—whether or not they are. Likewise, we judge them, trying to bring them down to the level we think we're at.

I believe when we have settled once and for all the question of our own acceptability and mental stability, we no longer look at others and wonder about them. We no longer fear judgment, because we believe in ourselves. We are free to *enjoy* others.

But the most beautiful way in which I see the Holy Spirit placing the fruit of joy in our lives is through the uniqueness he has given to each of us. From the very moment I knew Christ, I began to be aware of a special kind of worth. If he could come to live in me, then I must have value. As self-acceptance has grown, more and more I have become aware of gifts and talents which are uniquely mine. More than once I've been staggered to discover I have done something which I never before believed possible.

For example, when my friend Patti asked me to write a poem for the mother-daughter banquet, I protested that I didn't think I could. Of all the things I thought I would never attempt, it was poetry. But I agreed to try. Strangely enough, I wrote a poem, which later was published, and was even reprinted twice. I haven't had such spectacular good fortune with the poetry I've written since, but it has been an enjoyable way to express a thought or feeling.

Another discovery about my uniqueness has come through being the editor of the church newsletter. Since I don't have a journalistic background, I was very skeptical about taking on such a task. The surprise has been that not only can I do it, but I seem to have a knack for it. I've had a barrel of fun thinking of ways to make it eye-catching and interesting each month. It's given me a feeling of my place in the church and great personal satisfaction. It will be an experience to cherish when the time comes to pass it on to someone else.

Joy builds in my life as I progress and continue to discover my uniqueness and what it means to be a child of God. Sometimes my joy bubbles and becomes an intense experience. More often it is the quiet confidence which undergirds my life because I belong to Christ.

6

Peace: A Bridge
over Troubled Waters

IN THE PLAY *Rosencrantz and Guildenstern Are Dead*, two young men sit on the sidelines of life, almost as observers. Finally they go to their death as a result of their nonparticipation. As a matter of fact, they knowingly carry their own death warrants to Caesar. The play made a powerful impression on me when I saw it performed, and the story stayed in my mind for days, driving home its message of the need for involvement.

Later, I noted a similar theme in the newspaper cartoon strip *Funky Winkerbean*. Drawing up a "student profile," the counselor asked a teenaged boy whether he was a follower or a leader. The smile on the counselor's face was replaced by a look of utter dejection in the next picture. The boy had answered, "Spectator!"

I think it is easy to fall into the trap of sitting on the sidelines, becoming a spectator-Christian. All too often we choose to believe that the peace Jesus promised us means a blissful state of no-more-problems. At least that's the way I hoped it would be. I'd had enough trouble before I became a Christian, and I expected Christ to end all that when he gave me peace. But I've learned that Christ meant a different kind of peace when he promised it to us.

The Hebrew word for peace is *shalom:* not just freedom from trouble, but everything which makes for a man's highest good (William Barclay, *The Gospel of Matthew,* vol. 1, Daily Bible Study Series, p. 103).

It seems to me that it's escapist to want the kind of peace which comes from lack of participation in life. My friend Christy calls it being a "foxhole Christian." Because my life has been full of problems even as a Christian, I've had to recognize that I cannot cover my head and ignore them. I've come to believe that Christ means for me to acknowledge troubles and do something about them. The kind of peace he gives stays with me through the difficult situation.

There are two ways I can look at a problem: as something to get rid of or as a part of life. If I can face it as a normal part of life, I can work through it and grow as a person. Though the concept of a life free from trouble intrigues me, I know very well that I soon would be bored stiff. I need challenge in life, and perhaps this is why the Holy Spirit doesn't wipe away our problems magically, simply because we're his people.

The past year or so has been a struggle with my faith. I have felt far from God, sometimes nearly cut off. My Bible study and prayer have often seemed chores rather than filled with the delight of knowing my Lord. I've fumed and fussed, often irritated with myself and God over this state of af-

fairs. Yet there have been times when for a while I've come
to a breakthrough in the fogbank, and have known for myself some new truth about God.

Last Christmas, while I walked the beach, I suddenly understood with new clarity the kind of love it took for Christ
to come into this world. As I've gone through the year, even
though I've sometimes felt distant, I have been peaceful,
knowing the Holy Spirit is in this time with me. Lately, I've
realized that during this year of spiritual ups and downs,
my faith has become more strongly my own. It is not something borrowed from sermons and books and other people,
although I still benefit from those things.

One way the Holy Spirit has given me peace is through
hope, both in my daily life and for the future. It wasn't
easy to be hopeful when I was a new Christian, and I usually
wasn't. Once, in near despair over some problem, I asked a
friend how she managed to seem cheerful during difficult
situations. She told me she'd lived through enough problems
that she *knew* Christ would give her strength, and she held
hope for the worst situation. She added that this attitude
was something which had grown in her over the years. Since
then, I've learned my friend was right. As I look at the
cloudy sky, and know the sun still shines behind the darkest
of those clouds, I know also that Christ will turn the deepest
trouble into a hopeful situation. In fact, I've come to believe that the Holy Spirit sometimes gives us deeper peace
during trouble than during the easy days. Perhaps this is
because we more readily acknowledge our need for him then.

Finding hope for the future was also difficult. I had listened to too many radio preachers with their prophecies
that Christ was coming at such and such a time, and how
horrible it was going to be. It all scared me to death. Instead

of being able to look forward to Christ's coming joyfully, my reaction was that a door had closed in my face. I had felt that Christ was calling me to prepare myself for life on this earth for at least a while. But if these prophets of doom were right, why should I bother to do anything? What good was it to prepare for something that wasn't going to happen?

Then I attended a class at church taught by Dr. Bob Laurin, a brilliant man and one of the finest Bible teachers I've heard. For me, the class opened the closed door of the future. Bob talked about the purpose of God in history and the character of Scripture, pointing out that sometimes the statements in Scripture don't mean quite the same thing today as they meant to the people of the day in which they were made. Culture, languages, concepts, and meanings of words are different. For example, to the Israelites, heaven was the equivalent of lying under a fig tree. Is that how we want to spend eternity? Heaven is probably a very different concept to us.

As we studied "the signs of the times" in the class, we could see that they have been occurring constantly ever since Jesus' time—wars and rumors of wars, famines, etc. Jesus told us to go on living and be ready for his second coming . . . but that *no one* knows the time. So his coming could have occurred at any time in the past, or could occur any time in the future. This class gave me both peace about the future and the desire to live my best for God. Now I am inside the once-closed door. My faith seems larger and more exciting.

Having this problem settled for myself gave me the freedom to question my beliefs. On the basis that my life is firmly and irrevocably committed to Jesus, I can proceed in

a new way. I don't have to be afraid. No one can take away
my commitment. When I face my faith with this attitude of
discovery, sometimes questioning whether or not my beliefs
are based on God's truth, it seems to hold more possibility.
I have a new vision of the vastness and holiness of God.

My attitude about each day is essential to my feelings of
peace. With Christ's help, I try to look at one day at a time,
or even a part of it if need be. Sometimes when I get up in
the morning and think about everything I need to do, I feel
overwhelmed. Then I find it helpful to break the day up
into parcels, and only think about what I'm doing in the
next hour or two. It works the same way if I am putting
together a sewing or decorating project. If I can do it a
little at a time, I don't get caught up in concern over how
the whole project will ever get finished. Usually I can't find
a chunk of time big enough to finish anything at one sitting,
anyway. When I papered Sharon's room recently, I put up
one or two strips a day. The house was a mess the whole
week, but I was at peace because I did not have to pressure
myself. Sometimes I clean house by parcels, too, particularly
with the heavier work.

It is also helpful not to dwell on what tomorrow will bring.
I have to trust tomorrow to God. Today is enough. I used to
spend great hunks of my energy thinking about what might
happen. When the children were babies, every cold became
pneumonia in my mind, every trouble a serious injury. I
could have spared myself a lot of anxiety if I just had not
worried about disasters which never came to be. Knowing
God is with me, I've learned to try to dwell in the present,
and I've gained peace. In the case of my children, I've also

been able to give them more freedom since I've been freed of anxious worry.

But the single most important factor for me in discovering God's peace has been discipline. Basically I am a very undisciplined person. I grew up motivated by external forms of discipline. I worked for rewards, such as good grades in school. The discipline I've found the Holy Spirit leading me to, however, is something which comes from within. I struggle with it, sometimes fight it, often walk away from it. But continually, I come back to it, knowing it is through this inner discipline that I will find God's true peace.

First of all, there is the discipline of doing God's will. Basically, I must first want to know his will, though sometimes I catch myself not bothering. But when I can desire his will, pray about it and think on it, he lets me know, usually either through a flash insight or a friend's words. I used to worry about this, because anything I wanted for myself I thought was not God's will. For some reason, I felt he only wanted to make me do what I did not want to do. But I've learned that more often than not, when I find God's will in a particular situation, it is the thing which will give me the greatest joy in life. As I live what is God's will, I find a balanced, stable life.

Another kind of discipline is setting aside time for myself. This is usually difficult, because there are so many demands upon my time. Even when the kids are in school, there are other things screaming for my attention. But I need quietness to make things right with myself.

There are many ways I've planned this time over the past few years. One is by an occasional time away. Twice I've gone to a motel for a weekend, all alone. The first time I slept almost the whole time. I also find writer's conferences and Christian retreats refreshing. While the schedule at conferences is usually a bit hectic, the change of pace is good, and I always skip enough classes to have time to think.

As a mother, though, I can't indulge myself very often in time physically away from home. So, most of my time is squeezed in between other things. I go to the beach, take the kids to a park where they go off to climb trees, get up early to have coffee on the patio, or take an evening walk around the block. When all else fails, as it often does, I take the phone off the hook and just hibernate right at home. I'm not sure what the phone company thinks about that, but if anyone really needs me they'll call back. Probably all I miss is a real estate or magazine salesman!

I used to try to schedule at least a whole day at home once a week. Now that I am working again part time and my children are at the age where they need to be driven for baton lessons, boy scouts, and a multitude of other activities, I don't often find an entire day at home. But I still think it's a fine idea.

One of the most difficult things to overcome in scheduling time for myself was guilt. It came to me in many forms, both out of my own concerns for work I could be doing, and from comments of friends who do not share my need. My friends have grown used to the idea, however, and as I've seen the positive results in my life, it's been easier to schedule the time without having to justify it.

Most important to a peaceful life for me has been the discipline of a daily devotional time. Again and again, as I have wandered away from this time spent with God, I've felt the need to return. Then I've known true peace as I've lived with it on a daily basis.

I struggled with the mechanics of this, however, until my friend Lou Evans gave us his pattern for a daily devotional at our church family camp. It's with his permission that I pass it on to you.

It begins with Bible study, which can be any kind of approach. I like to choose a book of the Bible, and read it in as many translations or paraphrases as possible. I read Barclay's Daily Study Bible Series along with the passage. In simple language and with great perception, William Barclay helps me to understand what I could not know on my own, such as background or word meanings. Then I go through each chapter of the book and write down insights about what this particular Scripture means to my daily life. It's work, but I tend to be a bookworm, and I find this intense study very fulfilling. The Scripture becomes a part of me when I've worked hard on it.

Next in Lou's pattern comes a devotional reading which stimulates one's thinking. While I had read many such books since becoming a Christian, I had not read any as a part of my devotional time until Lou suggested it. I found it helpful to do this, particularly with rather "heavy" books. While I may not want to start something for lack of time, I find that if I make it a part of my devotional and read a few pages or a chapter a day, I'm soon finished.

Then comes prayer. My prayers had always been halting and sometimes repetitious, but I found Lou's pattern helps me in talking to God. He suggests we begin with *praise,* as an act of will, because other attitudes cannot exist very long

while we praise God. Next comes *confession;* if God forgives
our sin, then we're able to forgive ourselves and no longer
have to labor under guilt which lowers our potential.

Petition follows, which is asking God not only for the
things we need but for something to give to other persons.
During *intercession,* we should pray for others. For me, the
others are my family, people who are on my mind, those I
have covenants with, and persons who have requested the
prayers of a prayer chain to which I belong.

After this, Lou suggests a time of quiet *meditation,* where
we listen to God speak to us. Then finish with a time of
confidence, placing ourselves in God's hands today . . . and
then relaxed, *live* the day ahead.

When I have followed this discipline for my daily devotional, the results in my life have been fantastic. I have felt
close to God and have known a deep sense of communication
with him. It has given an order to my life. Whether I have
my devotional time in the morning or later in the day, I feel
a sense of beginning my day at the real place of beginning—
with God. The rest of my life falls into place because I am
at peace with myself and with my Lord. I accomplish much
more and feel more energetic.

This concept of a pattern may sound legalistic. I do not
feel that way about it. Actually there is a great deal of
flexibility in it. If my time is short, I simply shorten each
part; if I have a longer period of time, I lengthen them. I
used to scrap either my study or my prayer time if I were
rushed, but I felt I had missed something. Now I don't omit
any part. While I occasionally have days or weeks when I
feel trapped by this pattern, I don't feel tied to it so tightly
that I must do it at those times. I doubt God wants grum-
bling Bible readers, anyway. During those times, I continue

to pray as I go about my activities. But each time as I have walked away from this disciplined devotional, I've turned around and walked back to it, because it has brought meaning and peace to my life.

The most rewarding part of the devotional for me has been the power of praise. It was difficult to begin praising. I had to look around me and really look for things and people to be grateful for. At first, there were more pauses than praises. But as I continued, it became easier and more natural. Persisting in it, I have found my whole attitude about life changing. While I focused on what I had to be thankful for, I began to see good in other persons and in all kinds of situations. I felt a tremendous understanding of the grace of God in the gifts he's given us and in his caring for us. While I had tried many times to adopt a more positive attitude about life, I had been unable to do so. But as I continued to praise God for the good things in life, something happened to me. I found myself possessing a totally new, grateful attitude.

Peace? Yes, the Holy Spirit gives us peace, and when he does, it is the kind of peace which carries us through anything we may encounter. Over the most troubled of waters, the bridge of peace he gives us is strong and will not fall.

We have no reason to be spectator-Christians. We are free to participate fully in life. By God's grace we are given hope, the strength and desire to discipline our lives, and a thankful attitude toward life. We *live* in peace. Praise God.

7

Patience: Establish Your Heart

BECOMING TRULY Christian is not an instant success story.

Yet how often I've condemned myself for not acting or reacting "as a Christian." I've made myself very guilty because I have not understood that to learn Christ's way of life is a process and not something which happens overnight.

Certainly part of the reason for my misconception about becoming Christian is the state of our society. Everything from cake mix to quick-drying paint gives us immediate results. I'm not complaining about these products, for I use and enjoy many of them.

Even my laboratory job is totally different from the job it was ten years ago. While we used to do tests "by hand," now we more often put the blood through a machine. A blood count which used to take about fifteen minutes now requires forty seconds. A machine called an ACA now spits out chemistry results in about six minutes. When the machines break down, though, I wish I had majored in engineering rather than in biology and chemistry.

Modern inventions simplify my life. But some of the instant thing seems to have rubbed off on me and what I expect of myself. I have become a demanding person, and I want results right away. When something doesn't happen *now*, my natural inclination is to think something is wrong with me. I become a failure. How easy it has been to transfer these cultural expectations for instant success to my experiences as a Christian.

Another cause for my ideas about Christian perfection came from the various churches of my childhood. To my young mind, it appeared that this perfection was what one took upon himself if he or she accepted Christ. *Never* to sin again seems a heavy load for an adult, let alone a child. And while it has been easy for me intellectually to say that I believe being Christian is an internal process in which the Holy Spirit changes me over a period of time, emotionally I have not been so convinced. Some of my previous experiences were strongly rooted in my emotions and not so easily shed.

For example, when I was fourteen, I went to a camp meeting as a kitchen helper. I was totally ignorant about camp meetings, but I knew what camp was. I thought I was going to camp—a dream come true—and I packed my suitcase with all the enthusiasm and anticipation appropriate for such an occasion. Since I lived in the country where swimming pools were nonexistent, one of the things I looked forward to most at camp was swimming.

Words are inadequate to express my disappointment when I discovered there was no pool at a camp meeting, either. I spent my days setting tables, clearing them, washing dishes —and in between went to church services and prayer meetings. Not too exciting for a kid expecting camp!

But during the services I felt strongly moved to go to the altar. Instead of the joy I should have known, I felt terrible. For two days I cried, and all the while, through my sobs, people kept telling me I had to go back and be sanctified. Then it would be OK. I wasn't even sure what they meant, but they told me what a sinner I was. A goody-two-shoes kid like me? Anyway, after this procedure of going to the altar twice, first to be saved and then to be sanctified, I was supposed to be perfect ever after, no longer a sinner. All the other girls gave up their lipstick as a sign, but since I did not wear makeup then, I had nothing to "sacrifice." I went home frightened about what had happened, and somewhat guiltily tried to forget what to me had been a very embarrassing experience.

For a long time I've wondered about this experience and what it meant to me. Although I could not discover that it produced much positive change for my life, I think it helped teach me that becoming a Christian involves something more than just being converted. However, it seems to me that sanctification requires more than one trip to the altar. Perhaps in a sense it requires a daily trip there—to an "altar" in the person of Jesus Christ himself. I've learned that Christianity is not what we look like on the outside—not what we take upon ourselves—but what happens on the inside as the Holy Spirit works there.

Yet one of the most difficult things for me to learn *emotionally* is to have patience with the new me. I keep wanting to be a "spiritually arrived" person. I look at friends who have been Christians for twelve or twenty years, and say, "Hey, God, look at that! Isn't it fantastic? Why can't I be like he or she is, God?" Other times, as I grow impatient with the process, I get very tired of being a Christian. Non-

Christian life would be so much easier, I tell myself, because I would not have to be concerned about how I act or what I do.

Then I think about learning to play tennis. I grew up with the deeply embedded belief that I was clumsy and un-athletic. Of course, I lived out my belief, and my body grew stiff as it grew taller. Teachers watching my awkward attempts to participate in gym classes only affirmed what I already believed. So, when about three years ago I decided to learn to play tennis, it took a lot of teeth-gritting and determination just to convince myself that I had as much chance to learn to play as anyone else. Then I had to spend hours practicing. It took me one whole summer to learn to hit the ball. And it cost a heap of money for lessons and equipment. While I am still no super player, I *have* acquired enough ability to enjoy the game. Not only did I learn to play tennis, but I discovered something about life which I can now apply to my Christianity: to learn, or to go in a new direction, takes effort, determination, faith in both my-self and God—and patience.

The same discovery applies when I'm working on some big decorating project for the house. When we put an addition on our home a few years ago, it was delightful to spread the family out a bit. And it was fun for me to choose fabric for draperies and to make them. But I worked on one win-dow at a time. That's the way it goes with being a Christian. Christ redoes my inner house one window at a time.

Too often my expectations of how Christ should act in my life cause me to be impatient with him. I saw this most clearly with my headaches.

Perhaps I should say headache, because it was just that— one eight-month-long pain in my head. It never ceased, and medicine did not ease my torment one bit. Some medicines were like the cure that's worse than the disease; one made me sleepy and another made me feel like I was floating. The pain began after I had been counseling for some time with my brother-pastor, Lou Evans. In fact, I was really beginning to believe I was finished with the closet cleaning, as Lou called it, because I had vented tons of hostilities on his understanding ears.

So, I was certain something physical was wrong with me, and I visited two or three different kinds of specialists, only to be given a clean bill of health finally by my doctor. I didn't believe him, of course. How could I be healthy and feel so rotten?

Daily I prayed for healing. In my better moments, I believed Christ would heal me miraculously, and in my lesser moments, I thought *maybe* he would. At my worst, I blamed him and shouted at him for not giving me what I wanted. I don't think I ever stopped hoping for healing, but it came in a much different and more difficult way than I asked or hoped for.

The healing came because I was forced by the pain and a mother's necessity to "keep going" to consult a psychologist. I did not have much regard for anyone with a title beginning with *psych.* I thought "they" were all a bit squirrelly themselves. Besides I felt a Christian shouldn't need psychological help, *if* he or she had *the* right relationship with God. It just killed my pride to walk into the waiting room and sit there, wondering what people thought about me for being there. (It didn't occur to me, *they* were there, too!)

I never have been more aware of the Spirit's timing in directing my life than during this experience. Dr. Richard

Cox, a psychologist and a Christian, had arrived in San Diego just the day before I called him, almost as if he had been brought here only for me. All my preconceived fears about people with titles like his were dispelled as I talked to him. He is a beautiful person.

But I still had more pride to swallow, and it was in admitting my headache was psychosomatic. In my distorted method of reasoning at that time, I would rather have had a brain tumor than have to admit I was neurotic. So, Dr. Cox passed me off to the hospital, where I took all the necessary tests. Finally, when I had to believe there was no physical cause, I cried. I may be the only person in history who ever wept over *not* having a brain tumor. But I left his office that day knowing Christ could heal even a neurotic.

The following six months were agony as we talked about me and my past. But all through the excruciating process of therapy, I knew Christ's power was with me, and it gave me peace and a strange kind of joy. As I began to understand myself, I knew something had to change. I did not want to be an emotional cripple the rest of my life. Once I told Dr. Cox that I wanted to walk out his door some day and never come back, as a patient. And I think part of the reason I was able to do it was because he wanted me to, also. I had known people who had undergone therapy for years, with no apparent change. I did not want to be in that situation.

Thanks to the goodness of the Lord, I was not left to that. When I began to see the necessity for change, I would not have had the power to change had I been left to my own resources. Change for me meant I had a lot of forgiving to do—both myself and other people—and a past to put behind me. It meant realizing I had the potential to become the person God created me to be, and deciding to let go of some

old habits of hate and hostility. With the help of the thera-
pist God sent me, and the power of the Holy Spirit, I began
to be able to sort through my life, discard the meaningless,
and begin anew. When the headache stopped, believe me, I
knew I'd been healed.

The beauty of the healing has been in what it has done for
me beyond getting rid of the headache. During the time of
therapy, I learned much about how to handle problems as
they arise in my life. Now, when I have a problem, I know
how to search out my feelings and the situation, then go on
to discover a solution. It has given me power to live my life
in a new direction. Now I can thank God that he did not give
me the instant healing I desired, for the one he gave me keeps
on healing me daily. While I won't refuse a miracle if God
chooses to give me one in the future, I'm going to try to
keep my expectations out of his way. He knows what is best
for me, and I'd like to be patient enough to wait for it.

Strangely enough, moving into psychological health gave
me an unexpected problem. I began to realize that when I
was feeling best about myself as a person, I felt most distant
from God. If the Holy Spirit had brought me to this state
of personal well-being, was he now simply going to walk
away from me?

I don't believe so. It was just that I was entering a new
kind of relationship with Christ. No longer did I need him
simply as an emotional crutch. Instead of being a big spongy
receiver, I had moved on to a point where I could begin to
be a giver. The relationship was moving out to include other
areas of my life; it would still include the emotional, but as
part of the whole. I don't yet understand all that this two-
way relationship implies, but I do believe I have been grow-

ing into a fullness of Christian experience which I could not have known without a healthy mind.

When I occasionally question for myself this process of growing into Christianity, and wonder if I'm on the right track, I think about the growth of my children and of the garden. After months on a plateau, one of the kids will suddenly seem inches taller. Just as I was writing this, Diane came to me with too much leg sticking out of her jeans, and said: "Hey, Mom, do I look like I'm waiting for a flood?" It's new-clothes-time again.

It's the same with my garden, when it decides to grow. Some time ago I planted sweet peas and eagerly awaited their sprouting. I was delighted when they grew two inches overnight. You can't see the growth process while it's happening, but only as you stand aside and look back on it. Thinking about this has helped me to be patient for the work of the Holy Spirit in my life.

I've experienced this need for patience for myself also, both as a person and as a mother. After my time of therapy was completed, the question arose for me concerning the meaning of being emotionally sound. I've mentioned something about this before in speaking of Christian maturity and admitting problems. But particularly, in the first months after I had stopped seeing Dr. Cox, I felt I should no longer have problems—I had finished therapy. But I did have problems, and that worried me for some time. Gradually I began to see that having a few troublesome situations popping up here and there did not mean I had to rush right back to therapy. Therapy had given me the tools to work out problems myself.

It took a long time before I could grasp the concept that health means not the absence of conflict, but the ability to handle it. Then, like the seedlings or the inches-taller child, suddenly I could believe my head was on straight. The knowledge came crashing into my life, as refreshing as a reprieve from cancer. I was okay!

As a mother, too, I've had to learn to be patient with myself. (Probably my children do, too.) One day during vacation when I shouted about something, Steve told me he'd be better off being in school. Well, that put me back a little, because there's nothing he dislikes more than school. My impulse was to sit down and condemn myself to the lousy-mother category. But instead, I picked up a piece of paper and listed the good I pass along to my children. It helped me to see that in spite of my mistakes, I do love my children and accomplish some positive effects in their lives. I've never come this way before. Being the mother of three young *persons* is new for me. So, I grow as they grow up.

Patience for others has come as I've learned it for myself. A couple of years ago, a woman I know felt called by God to run for public office. She's a turned-on Christian, and I was delighted at the possibility of such a woman being in a political situation. When she lost, it was a crushing blow to many of us, until we realized God's call may not have meant she had to win. Patient waiting on our part may show the good which came out of her obedience to his call. The witness for Christ she gave to all persons she spoke to was significant, if nothing else ever happens. But I believe some day she'll have a public office.

At a conference recently, I saw how often we Christians tend to be impatient and judgmental with others. One of the speakers had made some statements which really incensed a number of people. By the time they'd finished criticizing him, they'd sent him verbally to hell. I'd like to think that if

I should or should not go to hell, it would be by Christ's judgment, and not by my fellow Christians' impatience with my progress. It's helped me as I look at the mistakes of others to remember Christians aren't perfect. They're only people trying to live for God.

A crucial area of patience, I think, relates to what I demand from God in all kinds of daily circumstances. Recently, our new pastor, Hap Brahams, told us, "God has something better for you than what you now have." I wasn't feeling too swift that morning, and my sarcastic response was "OK, God. Where is it?" By the time I'd returned home from church, my whole life had passed before my eyes, and I could see for myself, anew, the "something better" God had already given me.

Romans 8:25 is one of my favorite verses: "If we must keep trusting God for something that hasn't happened yet, it teaches us to wait patiently and confidently"(LB). James said it a different way: "Establish your hearts" (James 5:8, RSV). Although James was speaking of the Second Coming, I think it applies to all of Christian life. I like to whisper it to myself: Establish your heart. Over and over again as I've gone along, I see that I can trust God with my needs. He *is* trustworthy.

For example, when I was a new Christian, I became quite worried about my baptism. I had been baptized as a teenager, out of a feeling of embarrassment, instead of out of commitment to Christ. This now seemed a sacrilege, and it scared me. But I was counseled by two of our pastors that it was OK, and even though I did not understand, I decided to trust God to let me know whether or not I should be rebaptized.

It was one Sunday about two years later, during the

baptism of several infants, that my answer came. I listened
as the pastor explained to the congregation that baptism is
the Lord's promise to us. He spoke for several minutes, relating baptism to God's promise to Abraham. Finally it
all made sense. My baptism was OK. It was more than OK,
because I could see that our great God had honored even my
youthful embarrassed attempt by his promise to me, fulfilled
by my later commitment to Christ.

Not long ago, as I read through the stories in the Old
Testament, I was struck by one particular insight I'd never
noticed before. God made promises, but instead of waiting
for him to fulfill the promise, the people tried to do it themselves. The women were especially guilty of this. Sarah,
rather than trusting God to give *her* a son, gave Abraham
her maid. God kept his promise, anyway, and gave Sarah
her own son. Likewise, Rebecca tricked Isaac about the
birthright of Jacob, when God had already promised he was
going to take care of that. She couldn't leave the matter in
God's hands. Crafty women.

This really spoke to me as a woman. It helped me to see
that all too often I try to lend God a hand he doesn't need;
or I try to rush him along, like a mother with a toddler. Yet
the Bible and all my Christian experiences have been teaching me that when God promises me something, he will give
it in his own time and in his own way. All I need to do is be
patient, trusting him.

Patience for myself, my Christian growth, other people,
and God himself, is an outright gift of the Holy Spirit, for
I had none of my own. The Lord never promised me instant
success. But he did promise a fruit called patience even to
impatient Jan.

8

Kindness:
Let Kindness Be My Rule

IT'S POSSIBLE to be a model of human goodness without possessing an ounce of kindness.

I know this because I used to be a model good guy. To other people I seemed nice. But my goodness did not arise out of the desire to be kind. It came about through the repression of my true feelings.

While on the outside I appeared calm and pleasant to even those who sometimes derided me, I seethed with anger on the inside. I was an easy person for others to be with, always agreeable and seemingly cordial. Inside I was critical and hostile. Because I could not live with this internal conflict, I traded away my health to pay for the mistakes I made in handling my feelings. Most of my illnesses during years past were caused by inner turmoil. Yet I had a deep-rooted obligation to be good regardless of what I felt. It was the only way I knew to earn the love of others, since I did not trust them to care about me just for myself.

With Christ's help, and the sure knowledge that there is very little natural kindness in me, I've learned that true goodness is not something I do out of obligation. Real fruit-of-the-Spirit kindness grows out of wanting to be kind. And the desire to be kind comes only as Jesus Christ lives in me.

My husband, who knows what it's like to live with me, has often remarked that he liked me better before I became a Christian. My first response to this was defensiveness. I did not want to hear his words, which seemed a paradox to me. My conversion had made me unpleasant for my family to live with? How could this be? I struggled with this idea and argued with Neal about it—which only convinced him further that Christianity had ruined me.

It is true, though. My good-guy act *has* been ruined by Christianity. It does make me more difficult to live with. When Neal tells me I was a nicer person before, I have to admit I *was*. But I also have to recognize that it was an act, because I was not nice on the inside. I think I added to my sin of hatefulness by trying to cover it up from others, for then I added deceitfulness to the list. No longer can I be dishonest about who I am. It is no kindness to myself or to other people.

I readily agree that this has caused a struggle for my family. For the first ten years of our marriage, Neal knew me only as a yes-woman. I never argued back. How unfair it was to him and to the children, also, not to let them have a real person around the house. Instead I had given them a robot wife and mother. How much kinder it would have been if I had been real from the beginning rather than springing it on them later!

But the Holy Spirit takes us from where we are, not

from where we wish we could be, or where we see we should have been. Just so, he has been with me in this move from my phoney good-guy routine to true personhood. Where the real me is not kind and compassionate toward others, he's working on that, too. Sometimes I can see in me a deep-down concern for others, where I had none before.

During a mountaintop experience in which I felt at one with the Spirit, it became clear to me that real compassion for others comes as a result of closeness to God. All that week, as I went to the market, the bank, or the doctor's office, I could view the people behind the counter and desks as real persons. I felt as if something connected them to me, like a bridge of love. It was beautiful. I would like to have that much feeling for other people every day.

Maybe some day, as I live with God, I will know this as a daily experience. For now, I am content to know Christ is giving me the desire to be kind and compassionate. I have many opportunities to learn kindness as I go about my job at the hospital. People are often so frightened to be there, particularly children. It's easy to become hardened to their concerns and pains when you see them all the time. Perhaps closing off our sensors is partly self-protection: I find myself suffering as I'm aware of another's pain; how often, as I walk back to the lab from emergency room, I tremble all over and feel my stomach churning for the person lying there. But there is also a deep satisfaction in knowing I have a chance to pass on the loving compassion of Christ to the patients I serve. It gives a new dimension to my job.

As I studied the Gospel of Matthew, it seemed to me that kindness fits right into the fifth beatitude. "*Chesedh*, mercy, means the ability to get right inside the other person's skin until we can see things with his eyes, think things with his mind, and feel things with his feelings" (William Barclay, *The Gospel of Matthew,* vol. 1, The Daily Study Bible, p. 98).

This kind of sensitivity to other persons results in kindness. If we know why a person is behaving in a certain way, it helps us to be compassionate toward him or her.

When my kids were trick-or-treating a couple years ago, a lady on the next street said to them: "You children get out of here! I'm sick and tired of feeding the whole neighborhood." Well! As Steve said, it just about ruined the whole evening for the children. Normally, I would want to go and punch a person like her right in the nose; and I would certainly have some choice words to mutter to myself, or to her if I were brave enough. But something got through to me that evening, and I *knew* the kind of problems the poor lady must have suffered to cause her to respond to children so hatefully. It helped me to care about her. Also, an unexpected plus occurred because I was not angry with her: I was free to talk to my children about the experience and help them with their own feelings.

Spiritual growth groups in my church have helped me move toward sensitivity to other persons. As I've listened to others speak about their problems and their successes, it's helped me to know that there is something alike in the heart of each of us. Only by listening and trying to understand, can I know this. And knowing it, I can go on to be concerned and compassionate toward others.

I believe that perhaps the greatest kindness I can show another is to say truthfully, "I know what you mean. I understand." Often I have to let the other person see my struggles if I am to say that. It is, then, truly unkind if I try to hide myself as I really am. Probably this idea of getting under another's skin to understand, and being vulnerable enough to let others in to understand me, is one of the most healing things available to us as Christians. I've seen many persons blossom and grow into beautiful people through the kindness shown by a small group of people who have understood. One young friend I think of particularly was shy and insecure. Through several years of being with people who have given her *chesedh* understanding, she has grown into a happy, secure young woman, and found her way to a meaningful relationship with Christ.

One technique I find useful in showing sensitive understanding to others is "active listening." I learned about it while taking a Parent Effectiveness Training course. It works as well for adults as children. In active listening, one tries to feed back in his own words what the person speaking has said. It's helpful to the person who's listening, in understanding the feelings of the other. And it's helpful to the person speaking, in that it often helps him to articulate his feelings.

It takes some training to be able to respond this way. While I find I seldom am able to listen actively to my children, when I do, the results are good. The words "tell me about it" are effective also. Just yesterday, as Diane and I sat in the car waiting for Steve to visit the orthodontist, we talked for a long time. Or rather, she talked, and I tried to listen. Several things had been bothering her, some of them for quite a while. She felt better knowing I was making an effort to understand her. As we talked she was able to move from vague negative feelings about everyone and everything she could think of, to the point of expressing what was *really* bugging her.

An area of life influenced by the fruit of kindness for me has been morality. When I use the word *morality*, I mean in the broad sense of including the way I conduct all of my life.

The first matter I had to work out for myself in this concept of morality, as a new Christian, was just what it meant. I grew up seeing only the "rules" connected with various churches I attended. They were all "don'ts"! "Don't wear sleeveless dresses." "Don't cut your hair short." "Don't go to the movies." "Don't play card games." "Don't sew on Sunday." This was only part of what I heard. Vividly, I recall a preacher stomping back and forth across a stage, waving his opened Bible, and shouting about the evils of music.

As I look back, I am absolutely certain that these rules must have been only a minor part of what people tried to teach me. But to me, they became so major I could not see God over them. And while I could see the sense of God's Ten Commandments, I was so rebellious over the little rules of people, I even thought about not keeping God's laws. Fortunately, I never put my thoughts into actions.

During the week when I was trying to decide what to do about Christ, I attended a class at the church. There, the pastor gave a definition of sin which I'd never heard before: Sin is anything which breaks the relationship between God and man or between man and man. This new definition freed me to make the commitment to Jesus Christ. Suddenly I could perceive that he did not care about rules and regulations. He cared about me.

In a sense, this freedom was healthy for me, because I had to shake loose much of the garbage in my life in order to go in the new direction with Christ. Freedom gave me courage to do so.

But, in another way, I was too free, because I misunderstood my freedom. I was careless about hurting other persons. I was terribly *un*kind, often putting down other people in my quest for self-needs and in my determination to keep rules out of my relationship with Christ. Many things I did and thought make me feel rather ashamed. For example, I blew a small group because I could not understand why the other members did not have the freedom I had to speak their feelings. And during the search for personhood, I could have been a lot softer with my family, if I had not been so free.

Then, during a week-long Bible study held in our church, a visiting pastor spoke heavily on obedience to God and what we must do to have God fully in our lives. It seemed that all the old rules came rushing at me, and I saw red. I went home and prayed. The whole week my feelings were mixed with anger toward God and fear that I might have to have my freedom curbed.

Finally, as I prayed, peace came flooding into my angry, fearful heart. I was quiet. I knew I wanted God's will more than anything else—more than my freedom—even if it meant I had to agree to live by the "rules." So, I asked God for his will, somehow sensing that only then could I know what true freedom is about.

But I still believed God's answer to this kind of prayer was going to be filled with "don'ts." Surprisingly for me, all I heard was *do*. With clarity I saw Christianity as a way of life, doing God's will because I wanted to. I also understood I hadn't often let Jesus' Way be my way.

Now, I could see cause for morality in my life—a morality based on what I could *do* for God and the kindness I could show to other persons. James's words, "Don't just hear the Word, do it," became my goal.

While I sometimes still feel frustrated with the desire to

do wrong, I have both the strength not to rebel and the wish to show kindness as my way of life. I can see new reason behind God's commandments. He did not give them to us to frustrate us, but to help us. When I break his laws, if only in my thoughts, I make myself vulnerable to a ton of guilt. If I involve another person by my actions, I also put guilt on him or her. People simply aren't made to break those laws and live easily with the results.

As to the rules of people, I have not taken those upon myself. I still do not see reason for many of them. Why would God possibly care how I dress or wear my hair, as long as I'm reasonable about it? I'd rather think it's a real plus for Christ if I try to be attractive. And why not sew on Sunday, when sewing to me is fun? When God said to keep the Sabbath holy, I think he meant we should plan times of rest and recreation in our lives, not necessarily on Sunday. There are many people in the medical and other professions who have to work on Sunday, and I'm one of them. But I no longer have to rebel against the old rules, or to flaunt my freedom from them. I am free to decide what the Christian way is, using kindness as my rule.

It isn't easy. Often I find conflict over my desire to decide for the kind way, because my own wishes are usually selfish.

I struggled with this a few years ago when my first published article was about to be printed. It was a story which I wanted to tell because I knew it would help other Christians. But there were two or three persons who would have been driven to despair if they had read the story with my byline. They would have seen themselves in it. So, I was faced with the temptation to see my name in print along with my words —and the certain knowledge that I would be doing a cruel thing to other people in fulfilling my wishes. It was further complicated when the editor asked me for a photo. I could even have my face in print along with my name and words!

If I based my morality on kindness, on doing the Word, it was very easy to see what I needed to do. I could not risk using my name or my picture with the story: yet it must be told. As much as I wanted and needed the recognition, I finally had to put my desires in second place. I called the editor and asked him to please use a pen name with my article. It was one of the most difficult phone calls I've ever made.

But the Holy Spirit did not leave it there. As I hung up the phone, I was flooded with relief and joy. I knew I had done God's will in putting kindness for others ahead of myself. A short time later, my own desires were met when I sold another story which could be published with my name.

It appears to me that kindness is the fruit of the Spirit which I need most in my life. I need it each minute of every day as I respond to others, for I am not automatically kind in my actions and reactions. But Christ has brought me from phoney goodness and through misunderstood freedom to the place where I want his compassion to be seen in me. I'll trust him to take it from there.

9

Generosity: Pass It On

"PASS IT ON."

Those were the words of a friend when I asked how I could ever repay the gift of love and understanding given to me by other persons. My first reaction to feeling loved and secure was that I wanted to give back in similar fashion to the people who had helped me. It is easy, even fun, for me to be generous with those who have given to me. But as I tried to respond, I saw that those who had helped me did not need me with the same intensity I need them. Confused at first, I slowly began to understand that I could never repay them, nor did I need to.

As I've gone along, more and more I've perceived the wisdom in my friend's words. Increasingly, I see that my task as a Christian is to pass on to others what has been given to me. Christ has loved me and given me wholeness and the love of other persons, not only for my benefit, but for the good of the world. I turned to him for what he could give me, and he fulfilled those needs. Then as I could see beyond myself, he turned me about and gave me the desire to be a servant. If I can serve, there is a chain reaction which touches the lives of those about me, and others beyond them. The only way the world will ever know the full meaning of my life is in what I can pass on to others, or what I've done as my part of the chain.

It's a heavy responsibility, this idea of being a servant to others and the world. It's tough to think about, and harder to live. I'm not always sure I'm up to it. All too often, I'd like to retreat to my little shell of self-centeredness and let someone else worry about the servant bit. The Holy Spirit has a cure for that, however, and when I've begun to clutch things to myself, he nudges me on. In bits and places, through his urging, I've begun to be more giving. I've come to realize there is high hope for even a basically selfish person like me to someday be full of the fruit of the Spirit called generosity—so necessary to servanthood.

When I think about generosity in my life, I find the Holy Spirit working mainly in the area of the personal—giving myself to other people. I have always been a giver of material things. I naturally enjoy giving gifts to friends, or doing tangible things for them. I like making my church pledge and setting the money aside for it. No problem there. It is the real me I tend to hold back and keep to myself, and it's there Christ seems to be urging me to change.

Just as in other areas, if I begin to look at the whole concept of generosity—the vision of the future—rather than the reality of today, I get myself tied up in knots. I become filled with whys and hows and all manner of unanswerable questions. Faced with the demands of many and the needs of millions—if I look at the world picture—I end up feeling panic. How do I do it? How do I divide myself up to meet just the needs and demands I see in my family and friends? On days like this, I feel stretched out, aware of my limitations. I am like an octopus whose tentacles are busy with eight different kinds of prey just as some extra delicious morsel walks past. What does he grab it with?

Thus, one of the first matters I've had to resolve is priority for giving. It's meant I've had to sort through my life and my activities and decide what's really important. Of course, this means I need to begin at home, and most of my energies are here at this point in my life. This wasn't a difficult decision to make, but it sometimes has been tough to carry out.

Because my time spent beyond my family is limited, I've needed to think about what else I do. As a new Christian I became rather mixed up about this and got too involved in church activities and other services. My husband once accused me of going to church to watch the pews being dusted. Well, I didn't quite do *that*, but I did have my priorities a little confused before I learned to limit my outreach.

I soon found out, for example, that I am a lousy Sunday school teacher. Given a class of twenty-three eighth graders, I began with super-enthusiasm to tell those kids about Jesus. I studied about eight hours a week for class, planned a field trip, and enlisted guest speakers. What I didn't know was how to get the attention of fourteen-year-olds, and soon two or three of the boys were totally out of control—leaping over chairs, writing naughty words on the blackboard and switching lights on and off—while the rest of the class looked on with glee. Only with the timely help of the youth pastor did the church building survive my frustrated attempt to teach.

At least it taught me very quickly what I can't do. About the same time I learned, although not so graphically, that I am an equally bad den mother and Little League score-keeper. I had to begin to discover where my gifts and talents lie and to say no to people when they've called and asked me to serve in a position which I can't handle. Not only does it reduce the disaster area surrounding me, it saves my energies for the things which are really important. "Important" means choosing my specialties, such as the church newsletter, or my job, and doing them well, along with keeping my family happy.

My friend Anita has discovered what's really important to her in the area of giving outside her home. A former nurse, she was concerned for the patients at the local VA hospital, and contacted the chaplain's office to see what she could do. Anita now spends one day each week visiting persons there. For many, hers is the only visit they can look forward to. Their families are either far away or—in the case of one man—so repulsed by his illness they've stopped visiting. How important it must be to the people she visits that Anita has been able to sort through her life and focus in on one area of service.

One rather difficult thing for me to learn about generosity has been to tread softly. Sometimes in trying to love another person or to share myself, I've realized the other person doesn't particularly want to be loved or to relate deeply. I saw this most clearly in a group situation. It was one of the first groups I was in where my own problems were resolved enough that I could give something. Previously I had been a big spongy receiver in groups, and I was happy I could begin to help others. I could barely wait for someone to come up with a problem. One person in the group seemed to withdraw and appeared to be the perfect candidate for my

"generosity." I came on like a bulldozer wanting to be
friendly and helpful. It took a while before I realized that
I was only causing this quiet individual to feel threatened.
As a result I backed off, and though I haven't felt as if I've
done anything to help, I do think the relationship became
more comfortable once I was less pushy.

This and other experiences have helped me learn that
there is a limit to my responsibility. Once I began to find
enjoyment in the changes taking place in my life, I wanted
to pass it around. I knew The Answer, I felt, and when I
saw someone who had a similar situation to mine, I wanted
to tell him or her how to handle it. The only thing I forgot
was that, almost always, a person must find his own solution if it is to be meaningful. Thus I began to understand
the responsibility to change another person does not lie
with me, although I may be able to help if I am sensitive and
gentle. The responsibility lies with the person and with God.
On days when I want to change another person or tell her
how to solve her problems, I've had to learn to get down on
my knees and relinquish that person to the Lord. Christ has
helped me to perceive the difference between manipulation
of others and true generosity.

Almost paradoxically, I've discovered that asking someone for help is often giving them what they need. It lets
them know they're important. While Coke Evans was writing her first book, she asked me to read and react to it. I was
such a beginner writer that I'm sure my feedback couldn't
have helped her very much. But because she valued my
thoughts, I felt needed. Since then, I've tried to shake away
from some of my independent, I-can-do-it-myself attitude,
to ask people for help when I need it. By showing I need
someone, I can often open the door and give them a release

for their loneliness or insecurity. Besides, even the most fulfilled and secure of us still need to know we're needed.

Probably the most striking way the Holy Spirit has been teaching me generosity is through my children. I've always loved those kids, of course. But before I became a Christian, I tended to think of them as objects rather than people. When a visiting friend leaned down to speak to the children, I was struck by the fact that she talked to them with the same respect she would offer an adult. It was quite an insight to begin to recognize my children as persons. It's meant I've had to learn to be a lot more giving. I no longer can stand like a marine sergeant in front of the refrigerator door, doling out food. I've had to loosen up on rules and regulations, realizing the kids have wishes, too, and minds of their own.

They don't let me get by with stifling their freedom, either. They remind me, daily if they have to, that I am being overprotective and smothering them in their efforts to grow independent. One day when we were discussing whether to buy or pack lunches, I told them I just didn't feel like packing. They said they would pack lunches themselves, but I was worried they wouldn't get the proper balance of foods. Finally they convinced me to let them try, and they did a good job—though I spent the morning scraping peanut butter off the counter—and have often packed lunches since. While cleaning up peanut butter is not my favorite pastime, the incident helped me to understand more deeply the need for generosity on my part so my children may be free enough to learn and grow.

The person I am least likely to be generous with is myself. This ties in very much with motherhood for me, because it is in that area I most often feel inadequate. Because I had not treated my children as individuals early in their lives, I felt a lot of guilt, particularly after I became aware in therapy of the many ways a parent can harm children. I also have a desire to pass my faith on to my kids. How can I teach them about Jesus and the Christian way of life when I am such a stumbler myself—when I am only learning?

Then one day, I understood. I realized I had been loading guilt on myself when I didn't have to. With clarity, I finally grasped the fact that guilt is what I take upon myself willingly. I saw I had a choice not to do so. I realized my children will one day be able to look back and understand I did my best. Yes, I've made mistakes. I expect to make more in the future. But I found the freedom to forgive myself, to realize my human limitations, and to go on from there. At times I still have to willfully walk away from guilt feelings about my mistakes in mothering. But my basic outlook has changed from one of failure to one of hope. It's helped me to see the potential and the uniqueness of my children. I have been better able to let them find their talents and possibilities. And as for passing on my faith, I've learned to relax about it. I simply believe that one day Christ will be real to my children as he is to me. If I share as well as I am able, they will hear the message.

Another area of struggle toward self-generosity is my daily schedule. I often forget or push aside my need for rest, discounting it as unnecessary. Particularly on the evenings I work, I often get very little sleep. Yet, typically, I find myself expecting to do the same amount of housework, writing, cooking and such on those days as I do any other time. It is usually only when I begin to be snappy or out of sorts that I recognize my need to relax. If I feel grouchy or pushed when my family or a friend wants me to do something fun, then I know I *really* need to unwind.

As the Holy Spirit has led me through the struggles toward self-forgiveness, it's spilled out onto other persons. Two things have made me ungenerous with others in the past. One is that I have a memory for details. I can remember all kinds of little things other people forget, especially when someone has hurt me. The other is that I have tended to be intolerant of weakness in other people. I used to put certain persons on a pedestal, believing they were perfect. Then when I eventually perceived their weaknesses, it was a crushing experience for me as they fell off the pedestal.

Once I was able to forgive myself, I began to be able to relate to others on the basis of who they really are, seeing their weaknesses as well as their strengths, and accepting them as humans. Christ has helped me forgive, and forget, not only the details which I harbored and held to myself, but also the human failures which all of us have.

I saw this most clearly in a relationship with two persons I had known for years where I was struggling with remembrances of past injustice. In addition, I thought they were generally ugly people, personality-wise. As I prayed about the situation over a period of months, I expected Christ to change *them*. After all, they were the ones at fault, weren't they? I had never done anything wrong—not innocent me! To my surprise, Christ did not change them, but me. Since then, I have not felt the need to respond to the countless verbal jabs they've given me. My lack of response has seemed to break the cycle, and although they still make insulting remarks at times, they do it less frequently. And, oddly enough, I've begun to see the characteristics I once found ugly as rather amusing. I no longer expect them to change, and I can live in peace with them when we're together.

All this has spilled over into my home and my feelings

about it. While I used to be possessive, feeling very much
my "property rights," Christ has helped me to loosen up
and not hold my home to myself. I want it to be comfortable
for other persons. Some of my friends' houses are so homey-
feeling to me, I feel I belong to the family while I'm there.
When I lived with a doctor and his wife during college, I
felt at home the minute I walked through the door. And
while Margaret has moved since the death of her husband, I
could go back today and feel at home in her new place.
That's what I would hope others could feel here. While
I don't believe I've totally established an atmosphere of a
warm and open home, I do believe I am walking toward it,
with the help of Christ, as he removes possessiveness from
my life.

An aspect of generosity which I'd never thought of until
I met Myrtie Ann is the ability to accept what another
gives.

I met Myrtie Ann through my church circle. She lives in
a retirement home, and has no relatives. I could see her
loneliness, and did what little I could to relieve it. Although
I felt my efforts were minimal, they meant something to her,
and when she learned Steve wanted to go to camp that summer, she promptly provided a check to cover the cost.

My first impulse was not to accept her money. I felt unworthy. I also thought about other people who might need
it more, even though Steve could not have gone to camp
otherwise. As I talked to Myrtie Ann, and prayed about it,
I realized how much she wanted to give Steve this opportunity. If I refused to accept, I would be robbing Steve of a
camp experience and Myrtie Ann of a chance to be generous.
I learned that generosity is both giving and receiving grate-
fully.

Then of course, generosity is also evangelism—giving Christ away to others. I think anyone who knows Christ is eager to tell others about him. How can we be anything but enthusiastic about such a loving Lord?

I do believe, however, we have to be careful and sensitive about how we do this. A group of teenagers sat in a circle around my friend's child at the beach one evening, telling him about hell. This made me very angry with them, because I felt they were trying to scare the child into turning to Christ. Scare tactics or any manner of evangelizing which embarrasses others is wrong. I don't think Christ wants it like that. If we convince others of the love of God, the Holy Spirit will convict them of their sin in his own time and his own way. It's none of our business.

Rather, I feel the best way we can communicate our faith is through relationships and the way we live our lives. We can tell about Christ with enthusiasm, and that's part of it. We can set up programs to bring the Good News to others. We can have committee meetings, buildings, and all kinds of activities. But it is all just talk until we live it. People will not really believe in Christ until they see him with their own eyes, feel him with their own emotions, know him with their own minds to be real.

The most convincing way for me to give Christ away is to live with him myself so that he becomes such a part of me that people can see the reality of his love through me. This kind of evangelism makes me part of Christ's chain reaction of love, which will change the world.

Pass it on.

10

─────────────

Fidelity (Commitment):
A Sense of Belonging

F<small>IDELITY</small> . . . <small>FAITHFULNESS</small> . . .

Given a piece of paper and a pencil and a few minutes to define words such as these, I'd probably end up with a blank paper and a similar facial expression. Strange, because these are words I've heard all my life.

So, I'd run to my desk and grab my Webster's. There I'd find *fidelity* and *faithfulness* have just about the same meaning: maintaining allegiance; constant; loyal; devotion to duty. Each implies a continued, steadfast adherence to a person or thing to which one is bound by oath, duty, or obligation.

Next, I'd call my pastor friend Gordy Hess, who knows some Greek, and who owns a fantastic library which provides access to the original Greek word which Paul used: *pistis.* It means trust in others, confidence, a pledge, faith, and in the active sense, believing. It has a connotation of being trustworthy, dependable and reliable.

Then, as I put all this information through my own "computer," I would eventually discover what it means to me in my own language, and how it applies to daily life. In my everyday vocabulary, the word I would use to express the meaning of *pistis* is *commitment.*

As I then return to my Webster's, I see that commitment implies the delivery of a person or thing into the charge or keeping of another. It means a pledge or a promise to do something. One is bound by promise.

Yes, I like that definition. It makes sense to me. *Commitment* is my kind of word. To be bound by a pledge or a promise rather than by a duty or obligation speaks to me about the true sense of the word *pistis*. I think if I could sit down today and speak with the Apostle Paul, he would say much the same thing. For whether we name this fruit of the Spirit fidelity, faithfulness or commitment, I believe the sense of it is in being bound by our pledges and promises, in our relationship both to other persons and to God. It requires willingness to be at times the keepers of others, and at times to trust them to keep us. It means trusting God, with confidence, in our daily lives.

Commitment was only a word to me before I met Christ. Now it is filled with rich meaning as I think about the experience of knowing that other persons, through Christ, are committed to me. It is in the area of human relationships where I've learned the most about the Spirit's fruit of commitment.

The Greek word which is used in the New Testament to describe the special sense of community which Christians share is *koinōnia*—association, communion, sharing—from the root which means "to have in common." It means that we participate in a unique partnership with Christ and each other. There is a bond between us. This bond of commitment has given me a deep sense of belonging. I am at home, have found my roots in the church. This, to me, is the true meaning of the church as Christ intended it. The binding together of lives in fellowship satisfies the yearning deep-down in each of us to belong.

Sometimes as I sit in meetings with all the proper procedure—for which Presbyterians are famous—I hear so much which seems insignificant. Though I know organization is valuable in carrying out the church's mission, I think sometimes about the way the church was in the New Testament, and I wonder if we haven't partially misunderstood what Christ meant to give us.

For example, I was appalled in one meeting by the amount of time spent discussing whether or not we should send food to a family in the church who were passing through a time of physical crisis which caused financial and psychological stress. Some were afraid it would set a precedent and everyone would expect this kind of help in the future. As the discussion went on and on, no one could seem to agree. It was clear to me that the simple way to show Christ's love was to respond to the need with action, not words. I could not honestly let the matter end with just talk. I made a list of people who wanted to help with dinners, and gave each a date. As the food rolled in, that family knew love and commitment from the church which fed them spiritually as well as physically during the months of struggle.

Without others, I would not be the person I am today. To begin with, I probably would not be a Christian, because at first I did not understand the concept that Christianity is a process. I would have long ago become discouraged enough not to have made it without the support of my friends and their faith in my growth, especially on the days I couldn't believe. Because other people kept me in their care and let me know they would not leave me, I could see I had personal worth. Just the knowledge that other persons were involved with me gave me the security to risk changing. If I could add up all the support, listening, affirmation, and just plain love given to me through our church at La Jolla, it would weigh a ton. It is an ongoing thing, too. It doesn't stop when I feel good, or when I sometimes attempt to hide myself from it. It is there to stay, the foundation of my life.

The other side of the coin, of course, is that everyone needs this kind of commitment. Because others have shown me how, I am learning much about what it means to be committed. It isn't always so easy to stick by the promise we've made to another. But it is necessary, I believe, in carrying out the responsibility to care for others which we have as Christian brothers and sisters.

It means we must be reliable and dependable. Sometimes it's difficult for humans to respond with those character-istics. I've found in editing the newsletter that the worst place to work with people is in the church. It shocked me to discover there are many Christians I just can't count on to do what they've promised. I still find it mildly irritating. I believe the commitment the Holy Spirit gives us for one another challenges us to do what we say we will do, be where we promise to be, and to consider the time of others as valu-able as our own.

This kind of commitment also means that we are con-

strained to be trustworthy. To me, this says we must keep
the confidences given to us by another. When we are in a
sharing relationship, people sometimes tell us what they
mean only for our ears. I know from my own experience how
crushing it can be to have something repeated at the wrong
time. Once when I had a difficult problem, which I can't
recall at the moment, I told a friend about it. What a shock
it was, on Sunday morning, to have another person, a friend
of my friend, walk up to me and say: "How are you doing
with your problem?" It made me feel I had to be more careful what I say to whom. But more important, it taught me
to guard well the confidences my friends give to me.

The most difficult time I have maintaining my commitment to another person is during conflict. As I have already
mentioned, I learned very early to shut people out of my life
for hurting me whether they hurt me in the past, were hurting me in the present, or I sensed they might hurt me in the
future—I covered myself for all possibilities. I did it physically if possible, by not being around them. In relationships
where that was not possible, I did it emotionally. In this
way, I spared myself further injury, so I thought. It was
pretty bad news for relationships, however, and very dam-
aging to my health.

When conflicts began to arise in my Christian relationships, I began to understand, painfully, that I could no
longer shut others out. Often that has meant going to another person and saying, "I'm hurt." This means I have to
swallow a lot of pride, because I usually have a righteously
indignant feeling when I'm injured. But through the process
of talking it out, I've learned that very often my hurts are
simply caused by a misunderstanding. Once I felt a friend
was rejecting me because he walked away from me right in

the middle of my sentence. I couldn't sleep all night, and the next day I told him how I felt. When he explained how pre-occupied with his work he'd been the evening before, I could understand that his walking away was unintentional and forgive him for it. It saved a precious relationship which I might have ended otherwise.

In marriage, I've learned that staying through a conflict is all-important. As I've mentioned, I buried my feelings for years, believing I could not disagree with my husband and stay married to him. But I very nearly ruined our marriage because of this attitude. I had to learn the hard way that if my husband and I are real people with our own individual feelings and thoughts, we are going to lock horns every now and then. Pretending not to only causes psychological damage to the entire family. Besides, two people could live together forever and not know whom they married, unless they were honest with their mates. Realizing this, I no longer have to feel I am headed for the divorce court because I get angry, or because I don't like to repair cars with Neal. We have a long way to go in improving our relationship, but we both feel the commitment to stay together and make this thing work. While there may be a few people for whom marriage is a bowlful of cherries, I don't know many of them. Most of my friends would agree that it's a tough way to live. But the rewards of knowing another person deeply, as marriage uniquely permits, are worth the struggle.

This kind of commitment—living and sharing together in fellowship—goes beyond our human relationships, I believe. It helps teach us what God is like. There is much about God I don't think I'll ever understand until I get to heaven. But learning about commitment of others has helped me to see in some small way what God's love and commitment are like.

To be bound to each other in the church satisfies our longing for God, also, because we begin to know him more deeply as we see him working in lives all around us.

In my own church, I've seen commitment working most profoundly in small groups of people. Many of these are sharing groups, which we call Spiritual Growth Groups, although some are begun expressly for study and prayer. For whatever the reason begun, or the number of people involved, these groups have been healing to the lives of many in the congregation. The number is usually eight or twelve people, so everyone has a chance to participate. I've been in one group of only four, however. And one of the best experiences I've had was the day only Christy and I showed up for prayer group. I think praying together that day cemented our friendship in a way nothing else could have.

I asked Christy how she had been helped by groups. She replied that she used to think she was hollow inside. She was afraid to be too introspective, because if she looked very far, she might really find there was nothing there. For this reason, groups were threatening to her. But as she participated, and found friendships which continued beyond the groups, Christy has discovered she's been filled up by other people. It did not occur through confrontation or through any one happening. It was a process of affirmation. As she talked to others, they told her the good things they saw in her and the capabilities she had. She began to see there was something there, after all, beneath her skin.

I remember feeling surprised in a group when Christy said she felt inferior, and I shared my reaction with her. She has an ability to think and to speak her thoughts, an ability I admire. But I had never told her that because I thought she knew what a fantastic mind she has. But through feedback like this, Christy's discovered who she is. She's dared to look inside herself and to share and accept the good and the bad. It's refreshing to her that other people can know her and still like her. It doesn't surprise me at all, for she's one of the most likable people I know.

My friend Gerry's life has been changed by groups also. I met him four years ago when we both attended a theological conference. It was a bad weekend for me. I was suffering with my headache, and was very deeply involved with the negative things in my life. Yet when I was at perhaps my lowest point psychologically, God worked in Gerry's life in a positive way—a fact that intrigues me. When Gerry saw that I and a couple others there had problems, it was a shock to him. He thought he was the only person not entirely happy with his life. Through seeing this, and feeling the presence of the Holy Spirit in the room—I don't think I have ever felt it more strongly—he committed his life to Christ and began a new direction.

Since then, Gerry has seen his need for friends and has begun to be involved in more relational activities. Before his commitment, he told us, he used to make rugs, alone. He still makes beautiful rugs, but only for occasional relaxation. As a retired person, Gerry has a lot of time, and he is committed to the *koinonia* lifestyle of commitment and fellowship from now on. I don't know everything he does, because he doesn't flaunt it. But I've seen him down at the church driving people who have no cars, or delivering donated goods, or working in the office. He's served as an elder and a group leader. But, the most beautiful way he serves is in a prayer/healing ministry which many credit with saving their lives or speeding their healing.

Then, there's my friend Peg, who emphatically states that her marriage was saved by groups and by the commitment of other persons. Five years ago, she and Al and the children went to our church family camp, where Peg was in her first small group. One of our mutual friends, a soft-spoken feminine woman, told Peg very firmly that she had never before seen such an uptight, hostile woman. You'd have to know June to realize she could say *that* in a way which would not offend. But through the commitment of friends made in the group, Peg began to soften.

The next years were rough, with fights and short separations, and reconciliations. Peg says only groups held her and Al together in those years. Then, one day Peg decided she'd had it, and asked Al to move out. They were separated for ten long months. But during that time, a friend spent an entire evening with them each week, so they could speak to each other without fighting. Bob listened and loved them and devoted himself to getting them together again.

But Peg became discouraged. She finally decided the separation had been going on too long, and they were never going to make it. So, without telling either Al or Bob, she went to the lawyer and filed for divorce.

The day Al was to have been served the papers, he was in Washington, D.C. Bob, who was also out of town at that time, was awakened in the middle of the night in his motel room with a message: "Call Peg. Tell her she's going in the wrong direction."

He tried to go back to sleep, but couldn't. He got up and did some writing, only to be nagged by the message over and over. "Call Peg." Still he wrestled with the idea—a practical, logical man, he didn't believe God spoke in messages like this. And, of course, he did not know of Peg's divorce proceedings. He thought he was telling her to leave Al, since the last he'd heard they were still talking about getting together.

Finally, Bob could fight no longer. He phoned Peg and

said, "I don't know what you're going to think about this, and don't tell me now, but here it is—you're going in the wrong direction." And he explained how the message came.

Peg *did* know what she thought about it. She spent the rest of the night out on the balcony of her home, crying and praying. Mostly she felt angry with God for interfering when she had her mind made up. This added a whole new slant to the situation.

But a few days later, she hesitantly accepted Al's invitation to see Washington with him. They talked about the message and about Peg's plans for divorce. A few days later, we and other friends received a wedding invitation in the mail. Al and Peg began again by being remarried. They committed themselves to a new kind of marriage. And Peg says that very often, when she has doubts, or becomes hostile, the old message from God, "You're going in the wrong direction," comes back to her. Then she knows the divorce court is not a way out. Peg is in her marriage to stay, and the community helped put her there.

Commitment works. Whether you call it fidelity or faithfulness or commitment, the Holy Spirit has given us this fruit to bind us together in human relationships and in relationship to God. When we live in a home or a church where there is a willingness to be the keeper of other persons, lives are changed. People blossom like flowers as they find belonging and direction in life. Roots grow deep, and the yearnings of our souls for relationship are satisfied. This must be what Christ meant the church to be. In his church, we truly become God's people, citizens of the *koinonia* kingdom.

11

Adaptability: Who, Me ... Change?

ONE DAY when the prospect of change weighed heavily on my mind, I was startled to see a banner in the sanctuary which said: "Who, me . . . change?" At the bottom was a caterpillar and above it flew a butterfly.

It was such a small and simple banner that it's probably long forgotten by most who saw it. But it spoke to me because it symbolized much of the Christian life I had experienced until then. The contrast between the worm and the butterfly, to me, was remarkably similar to my life without Christ and with him.

While changes in my life since have not occurred with the rapidity they did during my early days as a Christian, I still find need daily for the fruit of the Spirit which J. B. Phillips, in his *Letters to Young Churches*, translated *adaptability* (Gal. 5:23). Others have translated the Greek word *praotēs* as *gentleness*. In his later translations, Phillips apparently changed his mind and called it *tolerance*.

Now, all this may sound as if *somebody* got confused. Not so, however, because the word *praotēs* has shades of meaning which can't be put into one English word. Barclay (*The Letters to the Galatians and Ephesians*, p. 56) calls it "the most untranslatable of words." To me, it's a fun word, and I loved the challenge of trying to discover its full meaning. At the end of my search, I still liked Phillips's original translation, *adaptability*, best. It seemed to sum up the richness of the word.

The Greek root *prau-* means teachable, flexible, softening, soothing, calming, suppleness, becoming mild—the ability to yield to change. In animals it means gentle-tempered or an ability to be turned or tamed. The *praotēs* horse has a gentle neck. He responds to a new direction with more power because he responds to the director. His spirit is submissive.

What beauty, then, this *praotēs* fruit adds to our Christian lives. As it grows there, we become more submissive to God's will. We grow to acknowledge him as *the* director of our lives and joyfully yield to each new direction, with more power for living than we had before. Adaptability is a necessity in our relationship to God.

It's necessary, also, in human relationships and for living in our world. In fact, I would go so far as to say that adaptability is one of the keys to life. Without it, we become cynical, hardened, and closed off within self-made prisons of fear.

That adaptability is necessary for psychological health is well stated by Lawrence Kubic: "It is the loss of freedom to change which marks the onset of the neurotic process."*

---

* Lawrence Kubic, "Role of Polarity in Neurotic Process," *Frontiers of Clinical Psychiatry* 3 (April 1, 1966), quoted in Thomas A. Harris, *I'm OK—You're OK* (New York: Harper & Row, 1967).

We see this illustrated every Saturday night if we watch *All in the Family*. Poor old neurotic Archie is uptight and afraid of anything new. No one is right except him. We all laugh, but there's a little, or a lot, of Archie Bunker in each one of us. We are mistrustful of other persons, afraid of blacks—or of whites if we're black—full of biased preconceptions and unfounded prejudices. We know we need to change, yet we fear even change itself.

We look about us, and change is all we see. We experience it in our churches, our schools, our clubs, everywhere. Whether or not we want change, we *have* it. Books like *Future Shock* tell us, too graphically, of the rapid changes in our society.

Even the Boy Scouts have changed. Who would have dreamed one of the bedrock organizations of our society would sense the need to be different? But, between 1970 and 1975, more changes will have been made in scouting than in the previous sixty years. For one thing, the name has been changed to just plain Scouts, and some activities include girls. Another major change is that scouts are now put into decision-making positions on councils. Rules for earning new ranks are different, several merit badges have been added, and so on.

If these changes in our society happened one at a time or a little more slowly, we could handle them. But they pile up, too fast, and soon we find ourselves staggered by them, perhaps feeling personally the effects of future shock—in the present.

But Christ offers us another possibility through the fruit of the Spirit called adaptability. We see things in a new perspective. We do not have to be afraid for our society or our world when we trust Christ. We may be concerned, yes, but the fear has gone because he is in charge. The knowledge that God controls history gives us peace for our society. We become free to be a positive influence for change.

This has been illustrated in the town of La Jolla where my church is located. Change has occurred in the racial situation because Christians have possessed enough of the Spirit's adaptability to overcome fear. In an organization called SOFA—Strongly Oriented For Action—fear has been replaced by action and even love as blacks, whites and Chicanos have worked together. They've established a nursery school for working mothers, have walked to provide funds to erect a community building for minorities, and are making strides toward providing low-income housing.

Neither do we need to fear for ourselves when we know Christ. We face personal change without fear, with submissive spirits. We learn through experience that the changes the Holy Spirit directs are for our benefit. In time, we even begin to welcome change.

I have experienced for myself that Christ can change fears to trust. I used to wake up during the night with my blood like ice water in my veins. Sometimes I had had a nightmare. Other times I simply heard noises. Each sound was someone who wanted to hurt me or my children. Once, nearly paralyzed with fear, I listened as the front door knob rattled. Finally, shaking so much I could barely move my legs, I got up and peeked out a window. I saw there my Siamese cat, left outside, jumping at the door knob. What a relief to see only that character cat when I had expected the worst!

My nighttime fears were lifted from me easily and simply, once I knew Christ was in control. It's one of the changes he's made for me, almost with no effort on my part.

Another fear I had was for my own safety. If I flew I *knew* the plane would crash. If we drove, I was certain we would have an accident. Every time I heard an ambulance, I feared for the life of my children. If we were out for the evening and the phone rang, I was sure the sitter was calling to tell me something dreadful had happened.

Little by little, one by one, these fears have been lifted from me as I've laid them at Jesus' feet. It's been a matter of habit, sometimes repeating the process a number of times, until I've known for sure that I am in God's keeping and no longer have to fear.

Eventually, I came to realize I no longer feared even death for myself or my family, though the pain of getting to the destination still bothers me a lot. (I mean, for instance, the pain of a person injured in an accident, the suffering involved in an illness like cancer, the psychological pain of the people left behind.) One night on the freeway, a car swung sideways in the road ahead of us and another car in the next lane swerved out and stopped to avoid hitting him. There was no place for us to go, no way to stop in time. I believe it was only the hand of God which somehow guided our little Pinto safely to a stop between the two cars, with just inches to spare. But in the seconds which elapsed before we stopped, I firmly believed that we would all be killed. In that moment I knew only peace, and that I was not afraid to die.

It is often not our fear of death, but our fear of life which keeps us from real living, though. Here is where we most need this fruit of the Spirit, adaptability. Daily we face small, sometimes large, changes. If we cannot change, we miss out on the good life God intended for us to have. We spend our days crawling along, wormlike, experiencing life only from the worm's-eye view, an inch above the ground.

But a life which is rooted in Christ has security and freedom to change, if we'll accept them. In fact, the first inkling that I needed to change, or *could* do so, came out of my relationship with Christ. It was as if he held a mirror up to me and said: "Look here. This isn't what I intended. Begin with it. Change." It was this kind of Spirit-led insight which challenged me to seek the counseling and therapy I needed.

Change isn't always easy. Because we're human we tend to pull back to ourselves and try to avoid it. There is the risk of the unknown. It's difficult to learn to trust Christ for that. We want to know what we're getting into. Also, there is often tension involved in change. Not many of us enjoy conflict and struggle, which are sometimes the by-products of change. But they are inevitable, just as in the chemistry lab there are inevitably some by-products that are smelly and undesirable.

So, sometimes we argue with God. We tell him we're not able, he's got the wrong person, or anything else we can think up which even sounds like an excuse. Moses did this: "You've got the wrong man, God." "They'll never believe *me*, God." "Send someone else." Like Moses, we hesitate, vacillate, and manufacture reasons why we ought not even to try. We list all the things wrong with us.

In doing so, we miss seeing the vision God has for us. He knows who we are and what kind of a butterfly we are becoming, the colors of its wings and how high it can fly. He will not give us the wrong directions.

How often I see this, particularly in my writing. I balk and refuse to yield to the Holy Spirit's direction. I get wrapped up in reasons why I should not write. They are such things as: "I am not a theologian, or a pastor, or anyone famous. No one will care what I have to say." Every time I've held back and refused to believe I am able, Christ has broken through my stubbornness with the reassuring words of a friend or through some new insight. He's kept me going, in this instance, in the same direction, even though my neck has not always been gentle.

The place where Christ has most profoundly taught me adaptability is in my church activities. It's probably fairly normal for a turned-on new Christian to be overzealous. I wanted to be involved in every class or function the church gave and tried to drag my husband with me. But I was so enthusiastic that I turned my husband away from the church. There were other factors involved for him, also, but the time came when I could understand what *I* had done. In a process which went on for several months, something in me began to sympathize with his point of view. Neal felt pushed out of my life. In his words I was "one of them" and no longer belonged to him.

Understanding his viewpoint, but knowing I could not give up my relationship to Christ, I began to pray. And the Holy Spirit changed my direction. He gave me the willingness to put Neal before the church. I dropped all activities, and we began going to church when Neal wanted to go, which wasn't often at first. It was difficult for me, even though I knew it was God's will, and I wanted to do it. And though I later resumed some activities—though fewer—this experience helped me to keep my priorities straight. I learned to minister to my family's needs first. It also gave me a stronger faith, for while I was away from other Christians a few months, I relied more heavily on Christ. And, finally, I believe it was the turning point in our marriage relationship, because I was able to put my husband back into the proper position in my life.

Perhaps one of the reasons adaptability is difficult for us to learn is because so many ideas are firmly rooted in us from childhood. I vividly remember someone telling me when I was small that my hair was "straight as a poker." I believed it all my life, until about a year ago when I looked in the mirror. I *saw* for the first time that I have slightly wavy hair.

My friend Jack related in a group how he was caught in a similar, but more serious, childhood misconception. When he was very small, he overheard someone say that airplanes should always land belly-side-up if they caught on fire. Years later, as a highly trained pilot Jack was flying when his plane's engine caught fire. His old childhood belief that he should land belly-side-up was the first thought to enter his mind. He had to fight it before he could perform as his later training had taught him. He did land safely, right side up.

These old ingrained, often false, beliefs which we carry around in our heads make it difficult for us to be flexible, even if we did not have the social changes to deal with. We need to be brave enough to try new things.

As I read Putney and Putney's *The Adjusted American*, about normal neuroses, I saw myself many times. Here, for instance: "Lack of talent seldom presents a real barrier to activity. . . . His [the average American's] perception of his capacities is distorted by his quest for indirect self-acceptance. He is inhibited by fear of failure, not by a total lack of capacity. It is not that he cannot, but rather that he cannot excel."*

"Rather that he cannot excel." This was me! How

---

* Snell Putney and Gail J. Putney, *The Adjusted American* (New York: Harper & Row, 1964).

many opportunities I missed in life because I was afraid I would not be The Best. For example, I didn't take art in college, even though I wanted to, because I was afraid I'd ruin my point average. Yet, good grades mean little to my life now. It's sad I could not have enjoyed school a little more.

But the Holy Spirit did not leave me with my fears of failure, even though failure to me was anything except an A. Slowly he's led me away from my need to excel in all I do. He's given me the adaptability I've needed to try new things, and I'm learning that enjoyment is much more important than excellence.

For example, I grew up believing I could not sing. A second grade teacher told me I was a monotone. Later, friends laughed at me, and that did it! I stopped even trying.

Two or three years ago, our church organist, Bob Slusser, challenged me about this. It was his belief that I had never learned to hear the notes. He worked with me, and once we got past my fear we discovered I am capable of hitting pitch and carrying a tune. I have a low voice range, which my teacher apparently could not deal with. While I haven't worked on it much, I now know I am able to teach myself to sing if I wish to invest the necessary time. I will not excel, but that no longer matters. Just to sing a hymn in church on key would be a joy.

I've experienced the same type of thing in the area of sports. Four years ago, we attended our church's family camp for the first time. It's a special event for our congregation—a week in the San Bernardino mountains—and we'd heard so much about it that we couldn't wait to get there. Part of the camp day is spent in spiritual activities, but much of it is free for recreation. The big game is volleyball.

Well, the last time I'd played volleyball with my stiff,

inflexible body, I'd nearly been laughed off the court. I wasn't about to have all my church friends see my humiliating clumsiness, and I wasn't going to risk having anyone laugh at me again. So, I did not sign up for the teams—only to discover someone else had put my name on the list. I was furious. I stomped out of the lodge and stumbled down the hill to my cabin, hot angry tears running down my face. For a long time I lay on my bunk, alternating tears with fist-pounding anger. Then I began to pray.

As I prayed, I saw how silly I was. The theme for the week was "Living on the Growing Edge," using Bruce Larson's book of the same title. Suddenly I perceived that if my Christian beliefs meant anything at all to my life where I lived it, they must be practical at a time like this. I decided if I were to take the theme of the week seriously, I had an awfully big edge on which to grow. Strangely enough, I learned to play volleyball that week. I wasn't the star player, but I enjoyed the game, and no one laughed at me.

It was a turning point in my life. I went home with the knowledge that although I would never excel in physical activities, I was able to participate without being humiliated. This discovery was the main factor in my decision to learn to play tennis—a game I now thoroughly enjoy. Just this week, as I found myself feeling frustrated because I cannot be a superstar on the tennis court, I remembered where I began. And I decided I've come a long way for a woman who could not even throw a ball across the net, let alone hit it, four years ago. I would not have been free even to try to learn if it were not for the Spirit's gift of adaptability.

When Christ comes into our lives and gives us this *praotēs* fruit of adaptability, we have a choice for the first time how we will act and react. We can view changes in our society in our old fear-ridden way, or we can live in confidence that God controls history, thereby being free to make positive change. And in our personal lives, the fruit of the Spirit called adaptability enables us to rise above our truncated self-images. We have a choice—to crawl along on worm level, or to opt for the butterfly.

I'll take my chances on the butterfly.

12

Self-Control: Freedom to Decide

In playing tennis, the most difficult thing for me to learn has been to keep my eye on the ball. Without concentration, it's impossible to hit the ball properly, if at all. My natural impulse is to look across the net to where I want the ball to go, which is the very place it doesn't go—then. To be a good tennis player, I must put all my energies into watching the ball and hitting it right each time. As the ball is returned again and again, I begin to grow tired and concentration becomes more difficult. I probably hit one ball out of ten properly. But I am given the opportunity to *try* many more times.

This illustrates what much of living the Christian life is about. As we approach each situation in life there is the opportunity to try to respond as a Christian. As we progress, we become more expert and more able to concentrate our soul's focus on being truly the Lord's person. Serving Christ and other persons requires control of self.

When I sat down to write this chapter, I had to first grapple with questions. Though I have seen the necessity for self-control in my own experiences and in those of others, still the questions arose: Why, if self-control is a fruit of the Spirit, do I need to put all my energies to it? If it is *self-control*, why do I need the fruit of the Spirit? Why doesn't the Lord just do it for me?

Though I'm not sure what the proper theological answer to such questions may be, I had to search for one which satisfied me. I believe it is tied into the fact that God chooses to give us freedom. He never forces us to act against our will. Rather he allows us to learn his way at our own speed and in our own blundering method. Only as we see our inability to control self and ask his help, does he step in with the gift of his fruit, which I think might be better named Spirit-self-control.

This God-given freedom is important to me because I grew up always needing someone to tell me what to do. I could not trust myself to make a decision, so I relied on others: first my parents and the school, later my husband, and then even some of my church friends. I searched constantly for an authority figure. It was only as friends began to refuse to decide for me that I could see I did not, deep-down, like being controlled by others. I felt manipulated. Most of what I did in my earlier years was for the response or reward of others, and not because I chose it.

In learning this about myself, I've grown to be a little pig-headed. I like to decide for myself, try things my way and learn for myself. I can't seem to believe anything unless I've somehow been involved in it or "been there." Whether this is an individual personality quirk or something inherent in all human personality, I don't know.

I do know, however, that although I desire to move beyond my self-centeredness, there are very few times I have found self-control easy.

One such time was when I stood in a line waiting to buy fabric. I was in a hurry, as usual, and irritated by the line. Then I noticed a woman behind me with a crying baby, and I remembered vividly what it was like to shop with a baby. Sensing her weariness as if it were my own, I did something very abnormal for me: I gave her my place in line, in spite of the added delay to my plans. It felt good, because I knew I acted in that moment a little like Christ would.

Usually, though, self-control is more like the tennis game, requiring all my energies. Though I have decided of my own volition that I want to be able to control my actions and responses in order to pass around the love of Christ, I am not often able to do so. It takes a process of seeing the need, making the decision afresh for each new situation, and then carrying it out. This is where "hitting the tennis ball" with concentration comes in. It requires practice.

Beyond that, it requires more than *self*. I cannot be a do-it-yourself Christian. Only as I am willing to allow the Holy Spirit to control me also, do I know the ability to have self under control.

Last week, as I returned home from family camp, I experienced this anew. We were asked to make a commitment at communion, write it out, and hand it to the pastor. I decided I wanted to come back home and be more Christian in the small areas of my life and in my responses to other persons. I find it easy to be Christian when I am in a camp full of Christians—but just let me out into normal life and watch me then!

I wasn't home an hour before I was muttering to my washing machine. Then I went to the market. On the way home a car drove into the exit from which I was leaving, and I snarled at the other driver. Later in the day I experienced a lot of hostile feelings toward a friend whose children had treated my children badly. Then, to top the whole day, my husband and I had an argument.

Well, I didn't have to be smart at all to realize I had blown the whole thing, regardless of my good intentions. So, I began again the next day with the same commitment, but with the sure knowledge that it will take many attempts and a lot of failure for each small success; and that I could only control myself with the help of Christ's power.

I've had to learn the same basic principle in many different areas of life. My attempts at self-control, combined with Spirit-control, appear to be the means to becoming more deeply Christian. This seems to be the growing edge for me.

Another area where I've had to learn this is my own personality. I am an aggressive woman. For a long time after I perceived this about myself, I tried to *change* it. It is unacceptable in our society for women to be aggressive, although Women's Lib is changing that idea somewhat. (I am not a Women's Libber, but I agree with part of what they say.) I was fearful I would be unfeminine if I remained aggressive.

After months of struggle, I realized I could not change this part of me. It is too basic a characteristic which helps make me who I am. I understood a need to control my aggressiveness, however.

This control has come in the area of my marriage, where I've had to learn to channel my energies in nondestructive ways. I used to take over, running the house and yard like some kind of an all-efficient superwoman. I cheated my husband of his chance to participate, made some of my friends feel inadequate, and exhausted myself. With the Spirit's help, I've learned to do my part toward maintaining our home, but admitting I need Neal's help and support. It's taken the drivenness out of my life, and freed me to use my energies in more creative ways which give me deeper satisfaction.

Aggressiveness affects the way I drive, also. Nothing brings out the nasty, hostile parts of me quite as fast as getting behind the steering wheel. I thoroughly dislike myself then. I talk to drivers of other cars, become irritated because they move too slowly, and generally ruin my day if I drive enough. It is on my "most needed to change" list.

The other day, I passed a neighbor on the way to La Jolla, about five miles from where I live. I drove my usual way, at the top of the speed limit, in and out of traffic, muttering all the while. My neighbor, driving 35 mph the whole distance, pulled up behind me at a traffic light. That experience taught me that the manner in which I drive doesn't even save time. And besides what it does to my disposition, it is a bad model for the children. It certainly is no witness for Christ, either. With his help, I am trying to change my driving habits.

Then, in my daily schedule, I've had to find a different kind of self-control from what I knew before Christ. I used to make lists of what I had to do on a given day. When a friend accused me of unrealistic scheduling, I told him, emphatically, that I never planned more for a day than I *thought* I could realistically do. I believed my friend was dead wrong, and that he was being hard on me.

The problem was, though, my schedule never worked, as

good as it looked on paper. The phone rang, or one of the children came home from school sick, or someone dropped by unexpectedly, and the schedule fell flat on its face. I began to feel possessive about "my time" and resented interruptions.

The breakthrough came one day when I realized that "my time" was not mine at all, but the Lord's time. If I belong to him, he owns my daily schedule. I did not throw out planning altogether, because to do that means a waste of valuable time. But my plans are now flexible. If I don't get something done one day, it will be there the next. If it's within God's will, the time will click together in ways I could never have dreamed up myself. I don't have to feel pressured about the tangible things I've accomplished. Instead I realize that people hold the most important place on Christ's list. When I do make plans, I've learned to allow "flexing time" for the unexpected but sure-to-come needs of other persons.

Another area in which I've found self-control necessary is in being a peacemaker. In such a situation, I've often had to step aside from my own feelings and thoughts and just listen and hope I can say something to help. I saw this most clearly when I received a phone call from an elderly lady. She was upset because a young friend had not been willing to carry out a project her way. I had barely hung up the phone when the young friend called. She was more angry than my elderly friend. There I was, very much in the middle. And I think the Holy Spirit was in the middle with me that day, because I was able both to understand each woman's feelings and to try to help them with the problem.

I'm learning that self-control is the key to handling emotions, also. Because I repressed them, particularly anger, for so many years, I didn't always know what to do with my feelings when I did come in touch with them. Negative emotions, like anger, were threatening.

One day on the tennis court I lost very badly. It wasn't so much the loss, though, as the way it happened, which angered me. My partner was so good that she actually stood in one place and returned every ball, while I ran back and forth all over the court and did everything wrong. I was furious, and stomped off the court as fast as I could because I knew I was going to cry. I ran past friends and did not acknowledge them. After my initial reaction had cooled a little, I was able to pray. I saw what I'd done to others with my unbridled anger. I had to backtrack and apologize. I realized it's okay and even necessary to feel anger at times. But it's important to be angry creatively, instead of pushing others around and insulting them with destructive actions. Creative anger can be expressed through talking it over with a friend, or if that isn't possible, through such ways as hard work.

One of the difficult problems of Christian commitment for me has been that I've had to learn to deal with depression. Perhaps that sounds paradoxical. But I was too numb before I knew Christ to feel either really down, or up. One of my friends, Bob, says he feels *worse* since he became a Christian. But he does *feel* now, and likes it. I believe part of the wholeness the Spirit has given me is a result of the awareness of my emotions, both good and bad. I'd rather experience only the good, but bad feelings are a fact of life.

While I don't always know why I'm depressed, I've had to find a pattern to deal with it, partly because my family depends on me and also because I've discovered the worst thing I can do is to give in to the depression. With Christ's help I'm learning to live hopefully through depressed days, and sometimes to find solutions. Here's the pattern I've developed:

First of all, when I feel depressed, I pray. I tell Jesus honestly how I feel, and if I'm able, ask his help. Then I think about it, and try to define what is causing my depression. If I do not find an answer rather quickly, I do not dwell on it. Too much thinking "going nowhere" only makes me feel self-pity, and deepens my depression.

I make an effort to be with friends. Sometimes I talk and find a solution through their counseling. This has been part of the beauty of small groups for me. Even if I am not currently in a group, I am still surrounded by a number of people who are committed to me, and who love me enough to listen when I have a problem. If there is no chance for sharing on a day such as this, just being with people, interacting, soothes me, and makes me feel a little more as if I still belong to the human race.

Then I try to do something physical. I scrub floors, or perhaps walls. With three children, it's no problem to find something dirty. Or, better yet, because it includes another person *and* physical exertion, I go out and play tennis. Something about making my body work keeps me going through the worst of days.

I also try to do something creative. The important part for me is to make it simple. If I choose a big task I'm not able to finish, I may bog down and increase my depression. So, I choose something small to make with my hands—maybe sew a T-shirt, or plant a flower, or bake bread. The creativity gives me a sense of satisfaction, and helps me to remember I am worthwhile.

The most effective means I've found to work out my personal depressions is to write. I sit down at my typewriter and put words on paper until I understand. Like the other things, it may not work. But often, the words begin to make some kind of sense to me.

One day when Diane was nine, she and I had an awful morning. She went to school in tears, and I plopped down on the sofa with my coffee, not far from crying myself. I began to pray, and realized I felt guilty. I moved to my desk and wrote out everything I felt about the morning. I was angry with Diane for blaming others for her own problems. Out of my words on the paper came my understanding: when I am unhappy about myself, I blame someone else— anyone who happens to be around, usually. And I saw very clearly why my little girl was striking out against me. Because Sharon and Steve needed attention critically at the time, Didi was getting almost none. She is a placid child, and I had responded to the demands of my two "noise-makers" and ignored her until she was forced to demand also. Through my writing, my guilt turned first to understanding, then to willingness to solve the problem. Then I knew. Diane only needed some "mommy time." I flew into my clothes, drove to school, and took her to lunch. She was delighted. And I learned something valuable concerning our relationship that day.

Still, there are occasional days when none of this works. (They grow fewer as time goes on.) I go to bed as depressed as when I arose. My whole world feels gray. I am separated from other persons almost as if a curtain of gloom were about me. It's difficult because there doesn't seem to be an answer. But on these days, I just trust Jesus. I simply believe in him. I know he is working in my life, and is not going to stop until he's finished. Knowing that, I can face even depression.*

An area I've struggled with very recently is heavy in a different sense from depression. In this case, the weight is on me physically. Up until about a year ago, I could eat anything. Occasionally I gained a pound or two, but it was a cinch to lose it.

Last year I must have passed the magic mark. In six months I gained ten pounds. Buttons and zippers were popping and I felt lousy. I pictured myself gaining at this rate for a couple years, and could see I was on the way to becoming a real chubb. So, I went to my doctor and began to diet. I lost the ten pounds in only three weeks.

But the place where I've needed self-control and Christ's help, has been in continuing to eat sensibly. To maintain my weight, I need to stick almost entirely to protein foods and vegetables and fruits. I've had to cut way back on bread, fatty foods, and empty calories. It is an area of daily struggle for me, requiring all my efforts and will power, and a lot of Spirit-control besides.

Self-control is necessary for the little happenings in life which we can't control, also. I've found it is often these little things which make my life miserable, because I fail to put them in the proper perspective. I cause myself all kinds of stress over simple frustrations. A line at the bank, a person who cuts ahead of me in any line, a grouchy neighbor, all can throw me off-balance. One day I realized how superior of me it is to think I can have control over everything which happens to me. I saw that I could choose, however, not to let

---

* This pattern was published in excerpt form in *Faith/at/Work,* Feb. 1973.

things control me and ruin my disposition. I think the way I face the minute-to-minute crises of life says more about how Christian I am than anything else. With Christ's help, I'm working toward self-control in this area.

Whether it is all the little things in life—where I seem to be right now—or in a large commitment to family or friends, I believe self-control is one of the most important factors in *being* Christian. It is only as I step aside from self-centeredness that I can help others and be a catalyst of change in their lives.

I know this from my own experience. The people who set aside their personal needs to minister to mine were the ones who showed me that God *is* love. Those people who would not leave me, no matter what I'd done, were Christ's servants to me. My life changed direction because they had Spirit-self-control in theirs.

When Christ walked up that long, long hill, carrying the heavy cross, and gave his life, he modeled for us the ultimate in self-control. But even our Lord needed God's power to face the sacrifice. In his great example we see a lesson for ourselves.

It's great news to me that God has given me freedom to put all my energies to work on learning self-control. But it's even better news that he has provided the power to help me get there. In this way, I can become truly Christian. Spirit-self-controlled, after the way of Christ.

Hearn, Janice W.

Peace with the Restless Me